ALTAR

TO

AN

UNKNOWN

LOVE

Rob Bell, C.S. Lewis, and the Legacy

of the Art and Thought

of Man

by Michael John Beasley

Rob Bell, C.S. Lewis, and the Legacy

of the Art and Thought

of Man

Published by:

The Armoury Ministries
www.thearmouryministries.com

Unless otherwise indicated,
all Scripture references are taken from the New American Standard
Bible®, Copyright © 1960, 1962, 1963, 1968, 1971, 1972, 1973,
1975, 1977, 1995 by The Lockman Foundation
Used by permission. (www.lockman.org)

Altar to an Unknown Love: *Rob Bell, C.S. Lewis, and the Legacy of the Art and Thought of Man*
ISBN: 978-1-935358-08-4

Copyright © 2011 by Michael John Beasley.

Library of Congress Cataloging-in-Publication Data
Michael John Beasley
Altar to an Unknown Love: *Rob Bell, C.S. Lewis, and the Legacy of the Art and Thought of Man*
    Includes bibliographical references and index
    Library of Congress Registration: TX 7-392-645
    4/28/2011

All rights reserved. No part of this book may be reproduced, stored in a retrieval system, or transmitted in any form or by any means – electronic, mechanical, photocopy, recording, or otherwise – without permission of the publisher, except for brief quotations in printed reviews.

For more information go to: www.thearmouryministries.org.

Dedication

To the memory of Martyn Lloyd-Jones

and all of Christ's faithful watchmen

of every generation

Ezekiel 33:7-9

And to my beloved wife Sandra

for her precious support, encouragement,

and love.

Deuteronomy 29:29:

"The secret things belong

to the Lord our God,

but the things revealed

belong to us and to our sons forever,

that we may observe

all the words

of this law."

Contents

Altar to an Unknown Love
Rob Bell, C.S. Lewis, and The Legacy of the Art and Thought of Man

Introduction: 9

Chapter 1 - The Art and Thought of Man: 21

Chapter 2 - The Greatest Love of All: 37

Chapter 3 - The Affections of Love: 59

Chapter 4 - The Freedom of Love: 85

Conclusion - A Solemn Message from Hell: 99

Appendix: 111

- *Love Wins - A Message of Uncertainty: 112*
- *Love Wins - A Missed Opportunity: 122*
- *C.S. Lewis And the Use of Language: 127*

Index: 139

INTRODUCTION

> *"...love demands freedom."*[1]
> *- Love Wins by Rob Bell*

On February 22nd, 2011, an online video was published advertising the book entitled, *Love Wins*, by controversial author and pastor: Rob Bell. As a result of this brief video, a firestorm of criticisms and summary judgments was broadcasted throughout the internet, even before the book was officially released. The pre-judgment deluge poured out by nearly all of Bell's critics rendered the conclusion that he had become a Universalist. Then, several pre-publication reviews began to enter the scene and, as the book's visibility continued to explode, Bell's publisher chose to advance the release date of the book from March 29th to March 15th. As more information about the book began to roll in, I became suspicious and wondered just how different his convictions might be from that of C.S. Lewis. Knowing something about the Emergent Church's affinity for writers like Lewis, I held on to my suspicions until I had a chance to read the book for myself. Much to my surprise, I was able to acquire a copy of *Love Wins* just a handful of days prior to its official release.

I consumed it that afternoon and was utterly disgusted.

Now the primary source of my disgust may not be what you think. On the one hand, Bell's treatment of the subjects of love, Heaven, and Hell was indeed disturbing on several fronts - the details of which are examined in the fourth chapter and

---

[1] Rob Bell, Love Wins - *A Book About Heaven, Hell, and the Fate of Every Person who Ever Lived* (HarperOne - An Imprint of Harper Collins Publishers, New York, NY, 2011), p. 114.

appendix of this book. However, the controversy surrounding Bell's book was especially troubling. The premature rush to judgment over what he had written effectively sidelined some very important issues. In the end, it is my contention that Bell is not a Universalist, *strictly speaking*, but that he does espouse a confused teaching that strongly reflects the views of C.S. Lewis and George MacDonald. The great oddity of the Bell controversy is this: nearly all of the loudest and most popular critics of Bell also happen to be some of the strongest advocates for C.S. Lewis and his writings. When I completed Bell's book, my disdain for what he wrote was nearly eclipsed by the bizarre treatment he received from many within the Evangelical community, especially in view of this yet unanswered question:

If Bell is worthy of such a stern rebuke, *then why not C.S. Lewis*?

This question is, in a sense, foundational to this book. For years now, I have had to respond to a number of prevailing influences brought about by the theology of C.S. Lewis and, therefore, Bell's similarity to Lewis offered little surprise. Lewis' popularity within modern Evangelicalism is profound and enigmatic. Even J. I. Packer addressed the enigma of Lewis' public appeal in his *Christianity Today* article entitled, *Still Surprised by Lewis*, September 7th, 1998:

> "The number of Christians whom Lewis's writings have helped, one way and another, is enormous. Since his death in 1963, sales of his books have risen to 2 million a year, and a recently polled cross section of ct [Christianity Today] readers rated him the most influential writer in their lives—which is odd, for they and I identify ourselves as evangelicals, and Lewis did no such thing. He did not

attend an evangelical place of worship nor fraternize with evangelical organizations."[2]

In his article Packer praises Lewis' literary achievements and influences, "gratefully" acknowledging his debt to the "Oxford don." However, his praise is strangely offset by the following admission:

"By ordinary evangelical standards, his idea about the Atonement (archetypal penitence, rather than penal substitution), and his failure ever to mention justification by faith when speaking of the forgiveness of sins, and his apparent hospitality to baptismal regeneration, and his noninerrantist view of biblical inspiration, plus his quiet affirmation of purgatory[3] and of the possible final salvation of some who have left this world as nonbelievers, were weaknesses; they led the late, great Martyn Lloyd-Jones, for whom evangelical orthodoxy was mandatory, to doubt whether Lewis was a Christian at all. His closest friends were Anglo-Catholics or Roman Catholics;[4]

---

[2] J.I. Packer, Still Surprised by Lewis: *Why This Nonevangelical Oxford Don Has Become Our Patron Saint*, (Christianity Today Online, September 7th, 1998).

[3] When speaking of his belief in Purgatory, he envisioned the purification process as follows: "I assume that the process of purification will normally involve suffering. Partly from tradition; partly because most real good that has been done me in this life has involved it. But I don't think suffering is the purpose of the purgation. I can well believe that people neither much worse nor much better than I will suffer less than I or more. 'No nonsense about merit.' The treatment given will be the one required, whether it hurts little or much. My favourite image on this matter comes from the dentist's chair. I hope that when the tooth of life is drawn and I am 'coming round,' a voice will say, 'Rinse your mouth out with this.' This will be Purgatory. The rinsing may take longer than I can now imagine." Lewis, C.S. (2002). Letters to Malcolm: Chiefly on Prayer (p. 108). Houghton Mifflin Harcourt. Kindle Edition.

[4] Lewis reveals his syncretistic perspective concerning Roman Catholic dogma: "There are three things that spread the Christ-life to us: baptism, belief, and that mysterious action which different Christians call by different names-Holy Communion, the Mass, the Lord's Supper." C.S. Lewis, Mere Christianity, (HarperOne, New York, NY, 2000), p., 61.

his parish church, where he worshiped regularly, was 'high'; he went to confession; he was, in fact, anchored in the (small-c) 'catholic' stream of Anglican thought, which some (not all) regard as central. Yet evangelicals love his books and profit from them hugely."[5]

The influence of Lewis is subtle, yet systemic. It is my contention that his emphasis on fantasy, his weakness in doctrine,[6] combined with his stunning popularity, has produced a host of problems for the modern church. Despite this, many continue to rely heavily on Lewis for solid doctrinal substance. In the case of Rob Bell's book, *Love Wins*, his one recommended source for the subject of Hell is Lewis' own book, *The Great Divorce*. Bell's citation of this work is quite interesting, especially when one considers Lewis' concluding remarks in his preface to *The Great Divorce*:

> "I beg readers to remember that this is a fantasy. It has of course - or I intended it to have - a moral. But the transmortal conditions are solely an imaginative supposal: they are not even a guess or a speculation at what may actually await us. *The last thing I wish is to arouse factual curiosity about the details of the after-world.*"[7]

Though Lewis here supplies an appearance of timidity regarding the "details of the after-world," his true beliefs

---

[5] Packer, Surprised by Lewis, 1998.

[6] This point is admitted by Lewis himself in various works of his: "...the questions which divide Christians from one another often involve points of high Theology or even of ecclesiastical history, which ought never to be treated except by real experts. I should have been out of my depth in such waters: more in need of help myself than able to help others." Lewis, Mere Christianity, p. viii.

[7] C.S. Lewis, The Great Divorce (Macmillan Publishing Co., Copyright 1946, New York, 1976 - Nineteenth Printing) pp., 7-8, italics mine.

actually belie this, as evidenced in his subjectively based convictions on Purgatory:

> "*I believe in Purgatory*. Mind you, the Reformers had good reasons for throwing doubt on the Romish doctrine concerning Purgatory as that Romish doctrine had then become. I don't mean merely the commercial scandal. If you turn from Dante's Purgatorio to the sixteenth century you will be appalled by the degradation. In Thomas More's Supplication of Souls Purgatory is simply temporary Hell. In it the souls are tormented by devils, whose presence is 'more horrible and grievous to us than is the pain itself...' The right view returns magnificently in Newman's Dream.[8] ...Religion has reclaimed Purgatory. *Our souls demand Purgatory, don't they?*"[9]

---

[8] Lewis' view of such a purgatorial reconciliation is indeed reflective of Cardinal Newman's *Dream of Gerontius:* "There let me be, and there in hope the lone night-watches keep, told out for me. There, motionless and happy in my pain, lone, not forlorn, - There will I sing my sad perpetual strain, until the morn. There will I sing, and soothe my stricken breast, which ne'er can cease to throb, and pine and languish, till possest of its Sole Peace. There will I sing my absent Lord and Love: - Take me away, that sooner I may rise, and go above, and see Him in the truth of everlasting day." Cardinal Newman's Dream of Gerontius (New York: Schwartz, Kirwin, & Fauss, 1916), p. 31. Such an influence of the doctrine of Purgatory came early in Lewis' life. When he was only fifteen, he wrote to his father, mentioning his reading of Newman's *Dream of Gerontius,* saying that it was "strongly written." Walter Hooper, ed., The Collected Letters of C.S. Lewis: Family Letters 1905-1931, (New York, NY: Harper Collins, 2004), p. 65-66.

[9] Lewis, C.S. (2002). Letters to Malcolm: Chiefly on Prayer (p. 108). Houghton Mifflin Harcourt. Kindle Edition, italics mine. Lewis also mentions his belief in Purgatory in his popular work, *Mere Christianity*. When speaking of God's salvific pursuit of men, he says the following: "Whatever suffering it may cost you in your earthly life, *whatever inconceivable purification it may cost you after death*, whatever it costs Me, I will never rest, nor let you rest, until you are literally perfect...As a great Christian writer (George MacDonald) pointed out, every father is pleased at the baby's first attempt to walk: no father would be

INTRODUCTION

Lewis' convictions often flow from the well of his subjective desires, yielding a complex maze of personal thoughts, feelings, fantasies, and philosophies; oftentimes leaving the reader with more questions than answers. This methodology frequently gives him the freedom to publish his theological musings, beneath the deep influence of George MacDonald, without offering many clear conclusions. A didactic procedure such as this gives him a form of protection from precise criticism; after all, it is difficult to hit a moving target. In essence, this largely reflects what Rob Bell does in *Love Wins*.[10] Both Lewis and Bell excel in such a pedagogy consisting of theological suggestions, inductive uncertainty, imaginative supposals, all interspersed with *some* dogma. With Bell, such a methodology is readily admitted in his book, *Love Wins:*

> "The ancient sages said the words of the sacred text were black letters on a white page - there's all that white space, waiting to be filled with our responses and discussions and debates and opinions and longings and desires and wisdom and insights. We read the words, and then enter into the discussion that has been going on for thousands of years across cultures and continents."[11]

Thus, the teachings of men like Lewis and Bell are rooted in precious little Scripture and, therefore, precious little certitude. Remarkably, *many* (not just Rob Bell) have employed Lewis'

---

satisfied with anything less than a firm, free, manly walk in a grown-up son." Lewis, Mere Christianity, pp. 202-203, italics mine.

[10] Bell draws very few theological conclusions in his book, *Love Wins*, however, Bell doesn't use fiction, instead he employs a series of questions and imaginative speculations in order to share his doctrinal musings. For a more detailed analysis of this, consult chapter 4 of this book, along with the appendix.

[11] Bell, Love Wins, p. X (Preface).

methods and writings in order to advance their own systems of theology. Moreover, there is a growing population of pastors and authors who lean heavily on Lewis' writings and have therefore continued to pass along this "Oxford don's" murky legacy. As it relates to the particular focus of this book, I would suggest to the reader that much of what is wrong with modern Christendom's treatment of the subject of *God's love* is deeply attributable to the influences of both Lewis and his chief mentor - George MacDonald. I would also submit to the reader that Bell's book, *Love Wins*, is the veritable *canary in the coalmine - yet few have noticed the warning-sign of its demise.* What we *should* learn from such a warning-sign is that Lewis' legacy is quietly dangerous, and yet in God's providence the Bell controversy has sounded a loud and needful alarm exposing this lurking problem within Christendom. Because of this, those who have openly promoted C.S. Lewis, while criticizing Bell, should reconsider the consistency and integrity of their actions. Strangely, Bell's fawning devotion to Lewis is quite similar to that of some of his harshest critics, making this conflict rather bizarre.[12] Those who aspire to be the watchmen of Christ's church are right to warn others about the teachings of Rob Bell; but they are wrong to ignore Lewis. In an absence of such warnings about Lewis, the church has been exposed to a number of compromised doctrines. This book will not attempt

---

[12] John Piper, a prominent and outspoken advocate of C.S. Lewis, has acknowledged MacDonald's mediated popularity in the current day: "...Lewis loved MacDonald and commended him highly." "...*largely because of this remarkable advocacy by Lewis, I think, George MacDonald continues to have a significant following among American evangelicals.*" John Piper, Jesus: The Only Way to God, (Baker Books, Grand Rapids MI), pp. 19-21, italics mine.

to cover them all, but this summary is offered to point out the broader scope of concerns surrounding Lewis:

1. Lewis had a strong deference towards fantasy and philosophical logic over Scripture.

2. He held to a purgatorial view of Hell which had the potential of reconciling sinners to God, postmortem.

3. He denied scriptural inerrancy.

4. He saw mankind as being innately good, and only partially depraved.

5. He held to a view of absolute human free will which clearly diminished God's freedom and sovereignty.

6. He had a view of the atonement that denied Christ's penal substitution.

It is not uncommon, nor surprising, that many who consume Lewis' writings end up reproducing many of his beliefs as well, *and Rob Bell is just another example of this.* And while there are several concerns about Lewis' doctrine that we could address, I have chosen to expose what I believe is the most prominent subject that has fallen beneath his influence: *the love of God.* Lewis' influence upon Bell's notions of love, in *Love Wins*, is striking. Bell's confident and repeated mantra that *love demands freedom* is reflective of Lewis' own teaching. Most who have criticized Bell have focused on his descriptions of Heaven and Hell, but, for myself, his obfuscations of the nature of God are perhaps even more stunning. In fact, only a deeply polluted view of God's love and grace could generate such a statement as this:

> *"[the better question is]...not 'Does God get what God wants?' but 'Do we get what we want?' And the answer to that is a resounding, affirming, sure, and positive yes. Yes, we get what we want. God is that loving. If we want isolation, despair, and the right to be our own god, God graciously grants us that option."[13]*

Really? Hell *is a gift of God's grace?* No serious student of Scripture would be able to read such a statement and remain indifferent. The violence done by Bell to the doctrine of Hell is bad enough, but what he does to the nature of God's love, in *Love Wins,* is simply astronomical. Bell's utter departure from biblical reasoning is breathtaking, and leads him into territories of thought that are disturbing. Clearly, his exaltation of human freedom is quite telling. The fact that he heralds the question of *human freedom* over *God's sovereign freedom* is deeply reflective of his admitted mentor. I am convinced that the entire Rob Bell controversy has provided a watershed moment and opportunity for the Christian community to give pause and reconsider the impact that C.S. Lewis has had, and continues to have, on the broader realm of Christendom. In addition, even though Rob Bell is mentioned here and elsewhere in the book, I should remind the reader that he will not be our focus. Instead, the focus of our study will be the collective forces that helped to produce Bell's seemingly innovative views of love and free will. Principally, we will examine the direct influences of C.S. Lewis, along with the indirect influences of George MacDonald, on contemporary understandings of the nature of God's love. More

---

[13] Rob Bell, Love Wins, p. 117.

specifically, we will consider how Lewis' faulty notions of *love* and *free will* yield the bad fruit of *subjectivism*. In doing so, it is my ultimate desire to warn the reader about these toxic influences. There is, in a sense, a *perceived novelty* that comes with the theologies of MacDonald, Lewis, and Bell; but doctrinal novelty should stand as a warning sign against the standards of God's ancient truth. J.C. Ryle was right when he warned his own generation concerning mankind's *natural desire* for philosophical novelty:

> "There is an Athenian[14] love of novelty abroad, and a morbid distaste for anything old and regular, and in the beaten path of our forefathers. Thousands will crowd to hear a new voice and a new doctrine, without considering for a moment whether what they hear is true.--There is an incessant craving after any teaching which is sensational, and exciting, and rousing to the feelings.--There is an unhealthy appetite for a sort of spasmodic and hysterical Christianity. The religious life of many is little better then spiritual dram-drinking, and the 'meek and quiet spirit; which St. Peter commends is clean forgotten (1 Peter 3:4.). Crowds, and crying, and hot rooms, and high-flown singing, and an incessant rousing of the emotions, are the only things which many care for.--Inability to distinguish differences in doctrine is spreading far and wide, and so long as the preacher is 'clever' and 'earnest,' hundreds seem to think it must be all right, and call you dreadfully 'narrow and uncharitable' if you hint that he is unsound!"[15]

Ryle's counsel is quite sound, and should be given serious consideration. There is a great danger that comes when we

---

[14] Ryle's mention of *Athenian love of novelty* refers to what is described in Acts 17 - a subject that will be addressed in greater detail in chapter 1 of this book.

[15] J.C. Ryle, Holiness: *Its Nature, Hindrances, Difficulties, & Roots*, (Charles Nolan Publishers, Moscow Idaho, 2001), p. XXIX.

embrace teachers for their popularity *above any other serious consideration.* Yes, C.S. Lewis is popular, but we must remember that truth is not ratified by the acclaim of men - *popularity in this fallen world is not necessarily a compliment.* My task here is to sound a warning to others in the wake of all that the Rob Bell controversy has uncovered. It was the Apostle Paul who understood such a duty of warning others as a faithful watchman.[16] Had he failed in any way to cleanse Christ's bride with the waters of God's Word; had he flinched from his duty of declaring the profitable doctrines of Scripture; had he refused to sound a warning in the face of the onslaught of error, then he would never have been able to say:

> Acts 20:26-27: 26. "Therefore, I testify to you this day that I am innocent of the blood of all men. 27. "For I did not shrink from declaring to you the whole purpose of God."

In order for us to maintain such integrity as that of the Apostle Paul, we must consider our need for Holy Writ above any other presumed "wisdom." Therefore, in the next section, we will seek out and acquire some necessary study-tools that will help us navigate our way throughout the remainder of this book. As we examine Lewis' treatment of the subjects of God's love and human freedom, we will encounter an admixture of needed warnings and exhortations. However, our ultimate focus will be on God's profitable Scriptures, over and above the errors of Bell, Lewis, and MacDonald. By the Lord's sufficient provision, let us be better versed in the former rather than the latter.

---

[16] In Acts 18:6 and 20:26, Paul was clear of the bloodguilt of others because of his faithfulness as a watchman of the church (see Ezekiel 33:6).

ALTAR
TO
AN
UNKNOWN
LOVE

CHAPTER 1
THE ART AND THOUGHT OF MAN

> *"...all answers deceive."*[17]
> *- George MacDonald in C.S. Lewis' **The Great Divorce***

The goal of this book is to address some of the contemporary forms of thinking regarding the subject of the love of God as influenced by C.S. Lewis. I can promise the reader immediately that my treatment of this matter will be quite brief, and I make no pretense of uncovering all of the nuanced layers of this subject as it relates to contemporary Christendom. Moreover, our focus will center on Lewis' influence, directly through his books, and indirectly through those who have followed his teachings. Yet I must narrow the margin of our study even further. Of the many foci that we could embrace within our study, three key emphases of Lewis will be central to our consideration of his doctrinal influence:

1. Lewis' views on Christian affections.

2. His exaltation of human free will.

3. His view of a potential purgatorial-restoration of those in Hell, postmortem.

As noted in the introduction of this book, there are other problematic and questionable views of Lewis that could be addressed, but the three aforementioned matters will help to focus our study, especially concerning their impact on the doctrine of God's love, respectively:

---

[17] Lewis, The Great Divorce, p. 124.

1. What is the nature and importance of God's love within a Christian's overall affections?

2. Does God's love impact notions of human freedom?

3. Can a loving God send sinners to Hell?

When one compares men like Lewis and Bell, their *similarities* of thought and methodology become apparent. Neither man is particularly tethered to the text of Scripture and the result is often a modified view of God's love for, and judgment of, sinners. Consider, for example, Lewis' treatment of the story of Esau in his book *The Four Loves*:

> "Consider again, 'I loved Jacob and I *hated* Esau' (*Malachi* I, 2-3). How is the thing called God's 'hatred' of Esau displayed in the actual story? Not at all as we might expect. There is no ground for assuming that Esau made a bad end and was a lost soul; the Old Testament, here as elsewhere, has nothing to say about such matters. And, from all we are told, Esau's earthly life was, in every ordinary sense, a good deal more blessed than Jacob's. It is Jacob who has all the disappointments, humiliations, terrors, and bereavements."[18]

Musings such as these radically alter the all-important warnings of Scripture, as in the case of the epistle of Hebrews:

Hebrews 12:15-16: 15. See to it that no one comes short of the grace of God; that no root of bitterness springing up causes trouble, and by

---

[18] C.S. Lewis The Inspirational Writings of C.S. Lewis: *Surprised by Joy, Reflections on the Psalms, The Four Loves, The Business of Heaven* (Inspirational Press, New York NY, 1994), p. 280.

it many be defiled; 16. that there be no immoral or godless person like Esau, who sold his own birthright for a single meal.

Thus, if we are now entitled to say that *Esau was not a lost soul*, then what happens to the crucial warning of Hebrews 12:15-16? An interpretive scheme like this breaks down language and word meanings in a very troubling way.[19] Such alterations of the nature of God's love and justice can transform entire volumes of theology. The impact that Lewis has had on these questions of theology is striking, and is greatly attributable to his appeal as a fiction writer. Here in America, the theological shadow of C.S. Lewis continues to span the continent, especially with the recent series of Disney movies based upon *The Chronicles of Narnia*. As well, in the church, it seems that more and more preachers are eager to cite Lewis in support of their theological positions. It would seem that, for most, Lewis' influential works of fiction provide the primary door through which his other doctrinal influences pass.[20] What seems to evade the attention of most is that those who consume Lewis' writings are also ingesting the doctrines of George MacDonald, whom Lewis calls his "master" as he says in his anthology to MacDonald:

> "...In making this collection I was discharging a debt of justice. I have never concealed the fact that I regarded him as my master; indeed I fancy I have never written a book in which I did not quote

---

[19] The author of Hebrews warns against those who are *pornos* [immoral] and *bebēlos* [godless] - *like Esau*. Lewis simply failed to give this inscripturated description of Esau any careful consideration. See also Romans 9:1-28.

[20] "Any amount of theology can now be smuggled into people's minds under cover of romance without their knowing it." C. S. Lewis, 9 August 1939, in The Collected Letters of C. S. Lewis. Quoted in Joseph Pearce, C.S. Lewis and the Catholic Church (Ignatius Press, San Francisco, 2003), p. 78.

from him. But it has not seemed to me that those who have received my books kindly take even now sufficient notice of the affiliation. Honesty drives me to emphasize it."[21]

More will be said about MacDonald's problematic views of Universalism, but for now we should note Lewis' sense of surprise that his readers were unaware of his strong literary "affiliation" with MacDonald. When reading both men, Lewis' fawning devotion to MacDonald is evident, which should be no surprise. In fact, Lewis offers us further insight into such devotion in his anthology to MacDonald:

> "This collection, as I have said, was designed not to revive MacDonald's literary reputation but to spread his religious teaching. Hence most of my extracts are taken from the three volumes of Unspoken Sermons. My own debt to this book is almost as great as one man can owe to another: and nearly all serious inquirers to whom I have introduced it acknowledge that it has given them great help—sometimes indispensable help toward the very acceptance of the Christian faith..."[22]

Perhaps the most obvious affiliation between Lewis and MacDonald is found in their broader deference towards *extrabiblical reasoning* and *inductive uncertainty*. Frankly, both men revel in it. In *The Great Divorce*, Lewis has a fictional dialogue with his master about the question of Universalism. The conclusion offered by MacDonald is one that heralds the merits of uncertainty:

---

[21] C. S. Lewis, George MacDonald, *An Anthology* (HarperCollins, New York 1946), pp. xxxiii-xxxiv.
[22] Ibid.

Lewis: "In your own books, Sir," said I, "you were a Universalist. You talked as if all men would be saved. And St. Paul too."

MacDonald: "Ye can know nothing of the end of all things, or nothing expressible in those terms. It may be, as the Lord said to the Lady Julian, that all will be well, and all will be well, and all manner of things will be well. But it's ill talking of such questions."

Lewis: "Because they are too terrible, Sir?"

MacDonald: "No. Because all answers deceive. If ye put the question from within Time and are asking about possibilities, the answer is certain. The choice of ways is before you. Neither is closed. Any man may choose eternal death. Those who choose it will have it. But if ye are trying to leap on into Eternity, if ye are trying to see the final state of all things as it will be (for so ye must speak) when there are no more possibilities left but only the Real, then ye ask what cannot be answered to mortal ears."[23]

As this narrative continues within the book, Lewis offers no *moralistic* refutation of MacDonald's imagined quip about Universalism, that *"all answers deceive."* Coming from a man whose imagination was most "basic" in his writings, this should be no great surprise.[24] It is this MacDonald/Lewis pattern of writing that has greatly impacted the church in the modern day through a *subjectivism* which heralds *extrabiblical reasoning* and *inductive uncertainty*. In many respects, the current trends found within the Emergent Church movement echo much of this. More recently, the heated controversy surrounding Rob

---

[23] Lewis, The Great Divorce, pp., 124-125.

[24] C.S. Lewis: "The imaginative man in me is older, more continuously operative, and in that sense more basic than either the religious writer or the critic." Packer, Surprised by Lewis, 1998.

Bell's book, *Love Wins*, has exposed more of these same influences, especially since his book is highly reflective of the same theology found in *The Great Divorce.* What is fundamentally exposed in all of this is the frailty and tendency of all men to herald their own thoughts above God's divine revelation. Many today are willing to believe that if men are religious and sincere, then their errors are cleansed by their better intentions, but this not the case. Humility is only genuine when it sits at the feet of God's authority.[25] Theologies that are based upon *extrabiblical reasoning* and *inductive uncertainty* have no foundation whatsoever and offer no substitute to biblical truth. To explore this truth further, we will shift our focus to the example of the Apostle Paul, who frequently confronted this very problem in his own ministry. Paul was not a man who reveled in uncertainty or philosophical speculation; instead, he directed his hearers to the certainties of God's Word. We especially see this when he ministered to the Athenians in Acts 17. When he travelled to Athens, he found himself surrounded by some of the world's greatest philosophers of the Greek tradition. At the mount called *the Areopagus,* many of Athens' finest would assemble for philosophical and theological debate:

> Acts 17:21: (Now all the Athenians and the strangers visiting there used to spend their time in nothing other than telling or hearing something new.)

---

[25] Isaiah 66:2: "For My hand made all these things, Thus all these things came into being," declares the Lord. "But to this one I will look, To him who is humble and contrite of spirit, and who trembles at My word."

Despite their intellectual renown, Paul observed and exposed the Athenians' ultimate bankruptcy. Though the people were "religious in all respects," their zeal and effort did not acquit their lack of genuine knowledge. Thus, Paul was "provoked" in his spirit as he observed "the city full of idols." Because of their condition, Paul didn't enter into some kind of compromise with the people; nor did he suggest to his audience that their worship had the *potential* of being acceptable as if they were *close* to the truth, instead, he revealed to them that their worship was utterly misdirected:

> Acts 17:23: "For while I was passing through and examining the objects of your worship, I also found an altar with this inscription, 'TO AN UNKNOWN GOD.' Therefore what you worship in ignorance, this I proclaim to you."

Amidst the vast assortment of idols on Mars Hill, the only meaningful object in their midst was that one benign altar which revealed the ignorance of the people. The statues dedicated to Zeus, Olympus, and Athena were hopelessly plagued with idolatrous philosophies, but the *altar to an unknown God* stood as the only *tabula rasa* upon which the Apostle could paint a clean portrait of the true God *whom the Athenians did not know.* His entire message filled the vacuum of their thinking, further underscoring their need for divine revelation - not philosophical speculation. Before concluding his sermon, Paul presented a very important truth regarding mankind's utter lack of wisdom and need for truth:

> Acts 17:29: "Being then the children of God, we ought not to think that the Divine Nature is like gold or silver or stone, an image formed by the art and thought of man."

CHAPTER 1 - THE ART AND THOUGHT OF MAN

Paul's argument would have been quite stunning to his audience. His introductory premise, leading up to verse 29, is that all men have an obligation to serve and worship God *because He alone is the creator of everything*.[26] Thus, creation was not the collective effort of the spirits and deities of the Graeco-Roman world, rather, the One true God created all things by His singular power and authority. This, of course, is a repeated truth found throughout Scripture,[27] and Paul offered this matter as a primer to his overall Gospel call. After stating this premise, Paul continued with two essential principles for all men, whether saved or unsaved, and this will serve as a crucial basis for our own investigation in this book:

1. Our Debt to God: "*We ought not* to think that the Divine Nature is like...": The primary verb in this statement is - *opheilōmen [we ought]*. This is a word that speaks of one's debt to another and, in the case of man's relationship with God, it refers to our divine obligation towards the Lord who is the Creator and Despot[28] of everything. What Paul states here is both crucial and powerful. He is clearly teaching that men *are not at all free* to entertain thoughts about God that He Himself has not revealed. Implicitly, Paul is indicating to us that it is Scripture, and Scripture alone (*sola Scriptura*),[29] that must

---

[26] Acts 17:24-28.

[27] Jeremiah 10:1-7; Isaiah 45:23; Rev 14:6-7.

[28] Jude 4: For certain persons have crept in unnoticed, those who were long beforehand marked out for this condemnation, ungodly persons who turn the grace of our God into licentiousness and deny our only Master [*despotēn*] and Lord, Jesus Christ.

[29] Paul's commitment to Scripture is quite clear. He was a man who reasoned, not from the oral traditions of men, nor from the intertestamental writings of the Jews; instead, he reasoned from God's revelation in the Scriptures: Acts 17:2:

be embraced in order to have *an explicit* revelation of the One who is, Himself, the *exegesis*[30] of the Father: Jesus Christ. When men wax eloquent regarding their own philosophies and subjective feelings about God's nature, they are violating their divine obligation towards the One who created them. Ultimately, man's lack of freedom to think of God as he wishes mirrors the principal commandments of the Decalogue.[31]

2. Our Natural Corruption: "...that the Divine Nature is like gold or silver or stone, an image formed by the art and thought of man." This text reveals the other side of the *drachma* in Paul's argument. On the one side (as previously noted), men are not free to think of God as they wish; on the other side of things, Paul reveals that men have this *sinfully innate tendency* to liken the infinite God to the finitudes of this fallen world. As Paul was surrounded with a full bevy of statues, images, and altars to the many deities, daemons, and spirits of the Graeco-Roman world, his references to *gold, silver, and stone* would have been extremely self-evident. Athens was filled with such statues, images, and altars made of gold, silver, and stone, and thus, his rebuke is quite clear. His point of instruction is piercing: all members of the human race have this natural inclination to craft deities after the *art and thought of man*. What a deep and penetrating blow this must have been to his proud audience, teaming with an abundance of artisans and academics. Their highest achievements of hand and mind were quickly thrown into the trash

---

"And according to Paul's custom, he went to them, and for three Sabbaths reasoned with them from the Scriptures..." See also: 2 Timothy 3:16, 17.

[30] John 1:18: 18. No one has seen God at any time; the only begotten God who is in the bosom of the Father, He has explained [*exegēsato*] Him.

[31] Exodus 20:3-5: 3. "You shall have no other gods before Me. 4. "You shall not make for yourself an idol, or any likeness of what is in heaven above or on the earth beneath or in the water under the earth. 5. "You shall not worship them or serve them; for I, the Lord your God, am a jealous God, visiting the iniquity of the fathers on the children, on the third and the fourth generations of those who hate Me..."

heap of human depravity by this one statement. Moreover, the words that Paul used in this statement are quite telling: *technēs* (art, creative inventions) and *enthumeseōs* (thought). We get our word *technology* from this Greek word *technēs*. With the worship and adoration of *technology* in our modern day, we see that mankind's problems never really change. The other term, *enthumeseōs*, is rarely used in the N.T. The root of this term comes from the word *thumos* (passion) and is used to speak of the *hidden musings and imaginations* of men.[32] What a pride-stripping moment this must have been to the Athenians! In addition, for Paul to make this declaration on Mars Hill, where the philosophers gathered to pontificate their supposed knowledge about the gods, reveals an abundance of boldness that is too easily missed through a casual reading of this narrative.

In all of this, the Apostle's teaching is quite clear: truth comes, not from the art and thought of man; instead, it comes, singularly, from God alone.[33] The relevancy of this truth is just as important for today, especially for those who may be tempted to be drawn to the art and thought of man over the authority of God's Word, and it is in this vein that we continue with the question of Lewis' ongoing influence in the present day. In his article, *Still Surprised by Lewis*, Packer offers an important admission concerning the central appeal of Lewis:

"The secret lies in the blend of logic and imagination in Lewis's make-up, each power as strong as the other, and each enormously strong in its own right. In one sense, imagination took the lead. As Lewis wrote in 1954: 'The imaginative man in me is older, more

---

[32] Matthew 9:4: And Jesus knowing their thoughts [*enthumeseis*] said, "Why are you thinking [*enthumeisei*] evil in your hearts?, Hebrews 4:12: For the word of God ...able to judge the thoughts [*enthumeseon*] and intentions of the heart.
[33] Job 28:12-13.

continuously operative, and in that sense more basic than either the religious writer or the critic. It was he who made me first attempt (with little success) to be a poet. ...It was he who after my conversion led me to embody my religious belief in symbolic or mythopoeic forms...'"[34]

The point of this citation is not to vilify all fiction and allegory, but to reveal the potential dangers that can accompany such methods of teaching - especially when such a methodology is *more basic* than the persuasive power of Scripture itself.[35] What Paul teaches us in Acts 17:29 is very important, and it is

---

[34] Packer, Surprised by Lewis, 1998.

[35] Lewis' love of fairy tales was strengthened through his belief that such a form of writing could reveal the "real potency" of doctrine. He also believed that such a form could help others to *feel rightly* about God Himself. Lewis described the process by which he developed such a deference towards this didactic form: "As these (fictional) images sorted themselves into events (i.e., became a story) they seemed to demand no love interest and no close psychology. But the Form which excludes these things is the fairy tale. And the moment I thought of that I fell in love with the Form itself: its brevity, its severe restraints on description, its flexible traditionalism, *its inflexible hostility to all analysis*, digression, reflections and 'gas'. I was now enamoured of it. Its very limitations of vocabulary became an attraction; as the hardness of the stone pleases the sculptor or the difficulty of the sonnet delights the sonneteer. On that side (as Author) I wrote fairy tales because the Fairy Tale seemed the ideal Form for the stuff I had to say. Then of course the Man in me began to have his turn. I thought I saw how stories of this kind could steal past a certain inhibition which had paralyzed much of my own religion in childhood. Why did one find it so hard to feel as one was told one ought to feel about God or about the sufferings of Christ? I thought the chief reason was that one was told one ought to. As obligation to feel can freeze feelings. And reverence itself did hard. The whole subject was associated with lowered voices; almost as if it were something medical. But supposing that by casting all these things into an imaginary world, stripping them of their stained-glass and Sunday school associations, one could make them for the first time appear in their real potency?" C.S. Lewis, Sometimes Fairy Stories May Say Best What's To Be Said, 1956, italics mine.

applicable to all men - *saved or unsaved*. The great danger facing every generation consists of this prideful temptation of straying from the sure foundation of biblical revelation for the myths and vain imaginings of men:

> 2 Timothy 4:1-4: 1. I solemnly charge you in the presence of God and of Christ Jesus, who is to judge the living and the dead, and by His appearing and His kingdom: 2. preach the word; be ready in season and out of season; reprove, rebuke, exhort, with great patience and instruction. 3. For the time will come when they will not endure sound doctrine; but wanting to have their ears tickled, they will accumulate for themselves teachers in accordance to their own desires, 4. and will turn away their ears from the truth and will turn aside to myths [*muthous*].

Paul's warning to Timothy is a timeless one, reminding us that what is most basic to the natural man is *mythology* and *human wisdom*, not truth. Thus, what the natural man needs is not more of what he desires; instead, he needs the Gospel which is the power of God unto salvation.[36] Those who fail to embrace this truth often fall into the trap of heralding the innovations of human thinking over the revelation of God. An important example of this is also seen in the Corinthian church. When the Apostle Paul wrote to the church at Corinth, he reminded them just how destructive worldly wisdom can be to the Christian's true *basis* of faith and power.

> 1 Corinthians 2:1-5: 1. And when I came to you, brethren, I did not come with superiority of speech or of wisdom, proclaiming to you the testimony of God. 2. For I determined to know nothing among you except Jesus Christ, and Him crucified. 3. I was with you in

---

[36] Romans 1:16.

weakness and in fear and in much trembling, 4. and my message and my preaching were not in persuasive words of wisdom, but in demonstration of the Spirit and of power, 5. so that your faith would not rest on the wisdom of men, but on the power of God.

Paul's concern for the Corinthians is very telling. Their affinity for philosophical eloquence and human wisdom was leading them to rely, not on God, but on their own "wisdom," and the evidence of their corruption was quite revealing. It revealed a pride, not in God and His wisdom, but in their own sense of "wisdom." Moreover, this core disease of pride and self-sufficiency revealed *a lack of genuine love.* This point of observation will be more fully developed in the subsequent sections, however the reader should remember that corrupted affections can only yield corrupted fruit; but genuine love bears the fruit of reverence for God and His Word. It is for this reason that Paul delivered crucial instructions on the centrality of love in everything:

1 Corinthians 8:1: Knowledge makes arrogant, but love edifies.

1 Corinthians 13:2: If I...do not have love, I am nothing...

Without a doubt, wherever pride waxes hot, love wanes. By the Apostle's simple teaching, it is clear that the true *sine qua non* of Christian affections is, in fact, the love that is *of God as revealed in Christ.* This important instruction was given to a church that desperately lacked such love and evidenced this deficiency through their exaltation of human wisdom. Of course their "wisdom" only produced the bad fruit of licentiousness, personal followings, abuse of spiritual gifts, rebellion, and a proclivity for doctrinal error. So loveless and scripturally vacuous was their conduct that Paul ended his epistle with two final charges concerning the centrality of love in all things:

1 Corinthians 16:14: Let all that you do be done in love...

1 Corinthians 16:22: If anyone does not love the Lord, he is to be accursed. Maranatha.

It is in this final chapter of 1 Corinthians that the Apostle makes one last appeal for the centrality of godly love *in everything*. Both of these statements closely resemble the foremost commandment (Mark 12:28-31) where we are called to love God and neighbor. Without such an affection of love, our efforts become like a noisy gong or a clanging cymbal (1 Corinthians 13:1). Without this first fruit of the Holy Spirit, all other thoughts and affections are spoiled. In the worst of all cases, those who have no love for God prove themselves to be the children of wrath no matter how zealous they are in their religious activities. In many ways, the Corinthian church is here with us today, especially whenever the message of God's love is polluted with human wisdom. Throughout history, many have falsely tried to separate the concepts of love and truth, but for the child of God, they are inseparable. Those who, in the modern day, revel in philosophies that are rooted in *inductive uncertainty* and *extrabiblical reasoning* reveal the same troubling affections and appetites which Paul himself confronted in his own day. None of us are immune to such dangers. Instead of holding to an epistemology of uncertainty which declares - *all answers deceive* - the believer's conviction is that which is found in Deuteronomy 29:29:

> *"The secret things belong to the Lord our God, but the things revealed belong to us and to our sons forever, that we may observe all the words of this law."*

What God has revealed will be cherished as genuine treasure by those who love Him.[37] Of course, there are mysteries that the Lord has not revealed to us - questions that are not answered in this life; yet those who transform most, or all, of the Bible into one indiscernible mystery reduce themselves to the bankrupt philosophy which declares - *all answers deceive.* A philosophy such as this takes the biblical revelation of God's nature and places it within the prison of human reason and logic, and this is no less true for the subject of God's love.

In the pages that follow, we will draw from the multiple lessons set forth in Paul's godly example. With these study-tools in hand, we will be able to proceed with our analysis of God's love and human freedom. Paul's example of ministry is crucial, for we see that he, *out of his love for Christ,* upheld no other authority but that of God and His Word. Without this, we may be tempted to pursue the frail and feeble *art and thought of men - but may it never be.* Those who claim to have faith in Christ have a *higher responsibility* to uphold this aforementioned divine obligation against the onslaught of human reason for this simple reason: *judgment begins with the household of God.*[38]

---

[37] James 1:17, John 14:21-24.

[38] 1 Peter 4:17: For it is time for judgment to begin with the household of God; and if it begins with us first, what will be the outcome for those who do not obey the gospel of God?

ALTAR TO AN UNKNOWN LOVE

CHAPTER 2

THE GREATEST LOVE

OF ALL

> *"This love [erōs] is really and truly like Love Himself."*[39]
> *- C.S. Lewis, The Four Loves*

In 1986 Whitney Houston popularized a song written by Michael Masser and Linda Creed entitled, *Greatest Love of All*, which contains the following chorus:

> *I decided long ago, never to walk in anyone's shadows*
> *If I fail, if I succeed*
> *At least I'll live as I believe*
> *No matter what they take from me*
> *They can't take away my dignity*
> *Because the greatest love of all is happening to me*
> *I found the greatest love of all inside of me*
> *The greatest love of all is easy to achieve*
> *Learning to love yourself*
> *It is the greatest love of all*

The popularity of this song is striking: it ranked as the number one hit in America[40] for three consecutive weeks. However, this should be no surprise. Within a culture that heralds the idea of self-love and self-esteem, the song - *Greatest Love of All* was received in its day with great enthusiasm since it espoused the idea that *the greatest love of all is learning to love yourself.*

Yet, is self-love the greatest love of all?

Whatever you may think of this philosophy of self-love, it has stood as the prevailing conviction throughout history revealing a very important truth about the nature of mankind: *we love to*

---

[39] Lewis The Inspirational Writings of C.S. Lewis: *The Four Loves*, p. 271.
[40] Hot 100 Chart, 1986.

love ourselves above any other. The way in which this self-love has been manifested and taught throughout history has varied to some extent; however, the essence of the message remains the same. In the present day, such self-love, often posited as *self-esteem*, has been elevated as the *sine qua non* for all aspects of life. Similarly, the ancient Greeks reflected this same form of thinking within the concept of *erōs*-love as that which was the chief of all others, respectively: *erōs (self-oriented love and ecstasy), philos (friendship love), philostorgē (familial love), and lastly agapē (general love and honor towards others).* For the Greeks, just as in the modern day, the *greatest love of all* was *erōs (self-oriented) love.* Thus, if one could send Whitney Houston back in time to the 1st century, she would have a number one hit just as she did in the 20th century.

Many readers of this chapter may not understand why it is that *erōs-love* has nothing to do with the biblical concepts of godly love and affection. This may be due to the fact that they have accepted the secular philosophy that *erōs*-love is the greatest. But this should be no surprise since this thought has been passed along as absolute gospel-truth for generations; and those who have passed along the baton of such thinking have done so, not only under the pretense of secularism, but more secretively under the pretense of Christianity. When passed on by the hand of the secularist, it is much easier to detect and resist; but when it comes under the pretense of religion, it is more difficult to uncover and expose. Throughout the years there have been many advocates of the importance of *erōs*-love; some famous; others who are less known. In recent years, one of the most famous advocates is that of C.S. Lewis, especially through his well known book *The Four Loves.* In his book, Lewis attempts to describe the aforementioned Greek terms for love (*erōs, philos, philostorgē,* and *agapē*), but in so doing he exposes the reader to precious little Scripture. Instead, Lewis admits, in the introduction of his book, that his approach would not begin with the template of God's love, but with mankind's subjective experience of love.[41] Lewis' commitment to the process of theologizing from human philosophies, experiences, and affections dominates his entire work,[42] and is made evident in statements such as: "'The highest,' says the *Imitation,* 'does not stand without the lowest.'"[43] Lewis' citation of Thomas à

---

[41] "'God is love,' says St. John. When I first tried to write this book I thought that his maxim would provide me with a very plain highroad through the whole subject. I thought I should be able to say that human loves deserved to be called loves at all just in so far as they resembled that Love which is God. The first distinction I made was therefore between what I called Gift-love and Need-love...I was looking forward to writing some fairly easy panegyrics on the first sort of love and disparagements of the second. And much of what I was going to say still seems to me to be true. I still think that if all we mean by our love is a craving to be loved, we are in a very deplorable state. But I would not now say (with my master, MacDonald) that if we mean only this craving we are mistaking for love something that is not love at all. I cannot now deny the name love to Need-love. Every time I have tried to think the thing out along those lines I have ended in puzzles and contradictions. The reality is more complicated than I supposed." Lewis The Inspirational Writings of C.S. Lewis: *The Four Loves,* p. 213.

[42] Before writing *The Four Loves,* Lewis wrote *Till We Have Faces, A Myth Retold,* which is based, in part, on the ancient Greek mythology of *The Tale of Eros and Psyche. Till We Have Faces* was published in 1956 and supplied the seed of thinking for his later work *The Four Loves.* In many respects, his deference for Greek mythology in the former work is quite evident in the latter. "In *Till We Have Faces* Affection, Friendship, Eros, and Charity are depicted in action; in *The Four Loves* they are analyzed." George Sayer, Jack, A Life of C.S. Lewis, (Wheaton IL: Crossway Books, 1994), Chapter 21 - Inspired by Joy, passim.

[43] Lewis The Inspirational Writings of C.S. Lewis: *The Four Loves,* pp. 214, 217.

CHAPTER 2 - THE GREATEST LOVE OF ALL

Kempis' work, *Of The Imitation of Christ,* is employed in his introduction to *The Four Loves* in order to suggest that our knowledge of the base affections of men upholds our understanding of the higher affections of divine love.[44] Yet, without a clear examination of God's divine love Lewis leaves himself without the needful standard with which to measure his personal thoughts about human affections. His resultant uncertainty, concerning the subject of which he writes, is partly revealed at the end of his introduction:

> "The human loves can be glorious images of Divine love. No less than that: but also no more-proximities of likeness which in one instance may help, and in another may hinder, proximity of approach. *Sometimes perhaps they have not very much to do with it either way.*"[45]

Lewis' statement raises an important question: how can we know if a human "love" is reflective of God's divine love, unless we first define the nature of *God's love?* Without God's standard; without understanding the nature of His love; or what is dear to Him, we are left with nothing but our own shifting sands of human affection. Thus, the frailty of Lewis' thinking is made especially evident when he comes to the section on *erōs–* love, and admits the following:

> "Hitherto I have been trying merely to describe, not to evaluate. But certain moral questions now inevitably arise, and I must not conceal my own view of them. It is submitted rather than asserted, and of

---

[44] "The highest does not stand without the lowest. A plant must have roots below as well as sunlight above and roots must be grubby...The human loves can be glorious images of Divine love." Ibid., p. 217.

[45] Ibid., italics mine.

course open to correction by better men, better lovers and better Christians."[46]

His conclusion in *The Four Loves* is even less certain. As previously noted, Lewis failed to begin with the benchmark of all genuine love - the love of God. Thus, after much ink and paper, Lewis makes this vague suggestion at the very end of his work, leaving the reader with more questions than answers:

> "I have included two Graces under the word Charity. But God can give a third. He can awake in man, towards Himself, a supernatural Appreciative love. This is of all gifts the most to be desired. Here, not in our natural loves, nor even in ethics, lies the true center of all human and angelic life. With this all things are possible." [47]

Then, without further explanation of what he means by this, he hastily ends his book:

> "And with this, where a better book would begin, mine must end..."[48]

Thus, what could have been Lewis' starting point in the discussion of love becomes his abruptly truncated ending. Throughout the book, Lewis is quite content to infuse his own subjective views about the nature of godly love and is rarely guilty of performing any scriptural exegesis. The result is that the reader is left with not much more than the poetic musings of a man. However, as Christians, we ought to prefer the clear *assertions* made by the Scriptures on this important subject. Such a thought takes us back to our aforementioned principle

---

[46] Ibid., p. 264.
[47] Ibid., p. 288.
[48] Ibid.

as derived from Acts 17:29, where we learned that all are under *divine obligation* to think of God's nature (including His love) in terms of *His divine revelation*, rather than by the art and thought of man. Most people reading this would agree, and yet, unfortunately, the application of this principle is often missed in the face of modern scholarship and popular philosophies. Unlike Lewis' popular book, *The Four Loves*,[49] we must embed our study in the Scriptures themselves and thereby seek to understand the Bible's emphasis on this crucial but oft misunderstood affection. Let us then begin with the Scriptures, examining what the Savior Himself calls *the foremost commandment*:

> Mark 12:28-31: 28. One of the scribes came and heard them arguing, and recognizing that He had answered them well, asked Him, "What commandment is the foremost of all?" 29. Jesus answered, "The foremost is, 'Hear, O Israel! The Lord our God is one Lord; 30. and you shall love [*agapēseis*] the Lord your God with all your heart, and with all your soul, and with all your mind, and with all your strength.' 31. "The second is this, 'You shall love [*agapēseis*] your neighbor as yourself.' There is no other commandment greater than these."

Our first observation of this text centers on the *kind* of love being heralded: it is *agapē*, not *erōs*. The significance of this will become more evident in the next chapter, but I must mention it here for the record. Secondarily, we must slow down and observe the principal emphasis of this commandment

---

[49] Lewis' enigmatic treatment of the subject of love reveals his lack of actual scholarship on the subject. This reality is only magnified by his slavish devotion to citing various poets, philosophers, and even his "master" - George MacDonald. Ibid., p. 264.

because, when we think of the foremost commandment, our minds tend to rush to verses 30 and 31. Yet, Christ's recitation of Deuteronomy 6:4-5 begins with an important premise in verse 29: "The foremost is, 'Hear, O Israel! The Lord our God is one Lord...'" Why is this portion so important? Firstly, the *principal command* within this injunction is actually - *Hear!* Hear what? Well, that's the foremost question within the foremost commandment! The truths that are revealed about God in verse 29 provide us with a crucial *archer's target* which cannot be ignored. Without such a target, no worshipper will be able to *hit the mark of genuine worship*. What is revealed in this important passage is the following: God is - *1. Our God; 2. He is the Lord; and 3. He is one.* Why is this so important, and what difference would it make if we were to ignore these details? Well, imagine a runner running *with all his might* in a race, yet he runs in the wrong direction, away from the finish line. The force and frequency of his effort does not rectify the fact that he is lost. Many in the modern day strive to love God with great effort, and yet, they too are lost. Thus, these aforementioned details are crucial, for they supply a precious description of the One who is the very goal and prize of every genuine Christian:

1. He is *our* God: This is no small statement! Exactly how is it that any sinner could ever call God *"my God?"* Well, the answer to this matter is supplied throughout the Bible, but all that we need to do is turn the page from *Deuteronomy 6* to the very next chapter for our answer: *Deuteronomy 7:7-8: 7. "The Lord did not set His love on you nor choose you because you were more in number than any of the peoples, for you were the fewest of all peoples, 8. but because the Lord loved you and kept the oath which He swore to your forefathers, the Lord brought you out by a mighty hand and redeemed you from the house of slavery, from the hand of Pharaoh king of Egypt."* The reader must not be tempted to think that these details, down to their last *jot* and *tittle*, are somehow insignificant - *they are not*. Those who have the ability to claim the Lord as *their God* can only do so by the free and unmerited gift of God's love. This principle is crucial and stands at the head of the entire commandment of love. The love that we are to give to God is the very love that *He initiated with us despite ourselves*. Many people go on throughout their lives worshipping the idol of a *deserved redeemer*. We might call this *treadmill religion*. Men, through their constant efforts and works will gladly believe that they deserve to call the Lord "*their God*" in view of the excellence and constancy of their religious persistence; but such a religion flies in the face of scriptural truth and belies the very essence of love itself. Such men may claim to be lovers of God, but they have not the love of God in their hearts.[50] For the child of God, his calling to be a lover of God is predicated upon the truth of God's *free and sovereign* love for the sinner. Without this understanding there is no meaningful way in which anyone could say - *the Lord is my God*.

2. He is the *Lord*: The words *God* and *Lord* might appear to signify no real difference, but this is not the case. The Hebrew term for *God* (*elōhiym*) was a generic expression and was also used to speak of the false gods of the nations. However, the word *Lord* (*Jehovah*) was given as God's peculiar name for the nation.[51] The principle being

---

[50] John 5:39-42: 39. "You search the Scriptures because you think that in them you have eternal life; it is these that testify about Me; 40. and you are unwilling to come to Me so that you may have life. 41. "I do not receive glory from men; 42. but I know you, that you do not have the love of God in yourselves."

[51] This thought of God giving the nation a personal, memorial name is reflected in Exodus 3:14-15: 14. God said to Moses, "I AM WHO I AM"; and He said, "Thus you shall say to the sons of Israel, 'I AM has sent me to you.' " 15. God, furthermore, said to Moses, "Thus you shall say to the sons of Israel, 'The Lord, the God of your fathers, the God of Abraham, the God of Isaac, and the God of Jacob, has sent me to you.' This is My name forever, and this is My memorial-name to all generations.

supplied in this is crucial. As we studied in Acts 17:29, God is not to be identified, described, or worshipped by the creativity, innovation, art, or thought of man; instead, the Lord is to be worshipped in view of His unique nature as expressed in His divine revelation. This truth flies in the face of the teaching of Rob Bell who believes that, apart from the Gospel of Jesus Christ, sincere men can and will be saved. Bell's mentor, C.S. Lewis, held the same basic view: *"The world does not consist of 100 per cent Christians and 100 per cent non-Christians. There are people (a great many of them) who are slowly ceasing to be Christians but who still call themselves by that name: some of them are clergymen. There are other people who are slowly becoming Christians though they do not yet call themselves so. There are people who do not accept the full Christian doctrine about Christ but who are so strongly attracted by Him that they are His in a much deeper sense than they themselves understand. There are people in other religions who are being led by God's secret influence[52] to concentrate on those parts of their religion which are in agreement with Christianity, and who thus belong to Christ without knowing it. For example, a Buddhist of good will may be led to concentrate more and more on the Buddhist teaching about mercy and to leave in the background (though he might still say he believed) the Buddhist teaching on certain other points."*[53] Despite Lewis' deference towards Universal Opportunity, the teaching of Scripture presents a very different picture. God's unique nature and identity is central to His

---

[52] Lewis' comfort with syncretistic thinking is evident in his writings. In 1960 Lewis travelled to Greece with his wife, Joy, along with some friends. Joy was dying of cancer and, in distress, Lewis expressed his desire to pray on her behalf in the following manner: "At Daphni it was hard not to pray to Apollo the Healer. But somehow one didn't feel it would have been very wrong-would have only been addressing Christ *sub specie Apollinis...*" Brian Sibley, <u>C.S. Lewis, Through the Shadowlands</u>, (Fleming H. Revell, A Division of Baker Book House, 1994), p. 148.

[53] Lewis, <u>Mere Christianity</u>, p., 209.

call of worship such that we are to have *no other gods before Him*.[54] This principle was not abandoned in the New Covenant, instead it was intensified through the revelation of Jesus Christ: *Acts 4:12 "And there is salvation in no one else; for there is no other name under heaven that has been given among men by which we must be saved."* This is no small tidbit of theology, and stands at the heart of all biblical teaching.[55] Christ alone is the way, and the truth, and the life, such that no man can come to the Father except through the *sole Savior* of mankind;[56] for there is no other name by which we must be saved. His unique identity also informs us about the nature of His love. The Apostle John teaches us a great deal about our calling to love God in view of His *uniquely expressed love for us: 1 John 4:7-10: 7. "Beloved, let us love one another, for love is from God; and everyone who loves is born of God and knows God. 8. The one who does not love does not know God, for God is love. 9. By this the love of God was manifested in us, that God has sent His only begotten Son into the world so that we might live through Him. 10. In this is love, not that we loved God, but that He loved us and sent His Son to be the*

---

[54] Exodus 20:3-4: 3. "You shall have no other gods before Me. 4. "You shall not make for yourself an idol, or any likeness of what is in heaven above or on the earth beneath or in the water under the earth."

[55] There is a recognizable pattern in Lewis' writing. He frequently instructs with a syncretistic flair. Rather than seeing a world of contrast between idolatry and true worship, all forms of religion provide gradations of truth within them, and therefore supply a meaningful *way* towards Christianity: "The question was no longer to find the one simply true religion among a thousand religions simply false. It was rather, 'Where has religion reached its true maturity? Where, if anywhere, have the hints of all Paganism been fulfilled?' With the irreligious I was no longer concerned; their view of life was henceforth out of court. As against them, the whole mass of those who had worshipped - all who had danced and sung and sacrificed and trembled and adored - were clearly right. But the intellect and the conscience, as well as the orgy and the ritual, must be our guide." Lewis, The Inspirational Writings of C.S. Lewis: *Surprised by Joy*, pp. 128-129.

[56] John 14:6: 6. Jesus said to him, "I am the way, and the truth, and the life; no one comes to the Father but through Me.

propitiation for our sins." Many men claim to love God with all their heart, but if they are not lovers of Christ, then they are sadly deceived and without hope.[57]

3. He is *one* Lord: This statement certainly seems simple enough. The Hebrew word for *one* is 'eḥād which primarily denotes the Lord's singularity, uniqueness, and supremacy above all other so-called "gods." Contextually speaking, this is what is emphasized in our passage. However, we should also note that this word, 'eḥād, affirms much more than the Lord's singularity; it also conveys the idea of *unity and diversity within that oneness.*[58] The bare implication of this idea is that God's own nature is *undivided* and without *contradiction.*[59] Thus, He is not the Author of confusion but of peace.[60] As we extend this idea to the broadest examination of Holy Writ, we must also remember that God is *one essence*, yet He subsists as three persons: Father, Son, and Holy Spirit.[61] Unlike the

---

[57] John 14:21, 16:27; Ephesians 2:12.

[58] R. Laird Harris, ed., Theological Wordbook of the Old Testament (Chicago: Moody Press, 1980), 1:30.

[59] Psalm 85:9-10: 9. Surely His salvation is near to those who fear Him, That glory may dwell in our land. 10. Lovingkindness and truth have met together; Righteousness and peace have kissed each other.

[60] 1 Corinthians 14:33.

[61] John Owen includes Deuteronomy 6:4 in his development of the harmony of the truth concerning God's *oneness* and *tri-unity*: "The first thing which we affirm to be delivered unto us by divine revelation as the object of our faith, is, that God is one...Deut. 6:4: 'Hear, O Israel; The LORD our God is one LORD.' A most pregnant testimony; and yet, notwithstanding, as I shall elsewhere manifest, the Trinity itself, in that one divine essence, is here asserted. Isa. xliv. 6,8, 'Thus saith the Lord the King of Israel, and his Redeemer of Lord of hosts; I am the first, and I am the last; and beside me there is no God. Is there a God beside me? yea, there is no God; I know not any.' In which also we may manifest that a plurality of persons is included and expressed. And although there be no more absolute and sacred truth than this, that God is one, yet it may be evinced that it is nowhere mentioned in the Scripture, but that, either in the words themselves or the context of the place, a *plurality of persons* in that one sense is

pantheon of conflicted idols and deities, who constantly fought with each other in the recited stories and myths throughout human history, the *one true Lord* has revealed the unity of His essence and divine will through the person and work of His promised Redeemer - Jesus Christ. The perfection of God's unified essence and divine will stands as a reminder of the relational unity between each member of the Godhead. Moreover, the fact that He redeems His children in order that they may enter into a *union* with the Father, through the Son, and by the indwelling Spirit, reveals the beauty of His triune love for His people.[62] Thus, the child of God can declare *"the Lord is my God"* because of such a unified love and purpose.

In all of this, we conclude that one cannot love the true God *rightly* apart from these aforementioned realities:

1. He is our God, not by our personal merit, but by His sovereign love.

2. He is the sole Lord over all, whose revealed person and nature is to be the focus of our affection and devotion.

3. As the one supreme Lord He is one unified essence, without contradiction in all of His attributes, subsistence, divine will, and actions.

Men who spend their days serving alternate deities, if even with all their heart, soul, mind, and strength, do so as a damnable exercise. Such a *treadmill religion* as this goes absolutely nowhere. The centrality of this foremost commandment will require us to revisit it again; but at this point, the reader *must*

---

intimated." John Owen, The Works of John Owen, ed. William H. Goold (Fakenham, Norfolk: The Banner of Truth Trust, Fakenham Press Limited, 1980), 2:381.

[62] Ephesians 1:3-14.

understand that the primacy of this text is established by Christ who called it the *foremost commandment*. His emphasis on this central affection is crucial, and should mold our thinking about all other Christian affections. Thus, God's love for us is given *freely* despite our *slavery to sin*; and the believer's new freedom is defined by the infallible grip of Christ's omnipotent love:

> 2 Corinthians 5:14-15: 14. For the love of Christ controls us, having concluded this, that one died for all, therefore all died; 15. and He died for all, so that they who live might no longer live for themselves, but for Him who died and rose again on their behalf.

Paul's statement about Christ's love is compelling. The natural man will recoil against Paul's expression - the love of Christ *controls* us - [*sunexei*], believing this to be *restrictive* slavery. However, the domain of God's infinite love is the truest form of freedom for the *bondslaves* of Christ. Thus, it is not burdensome[63] for the believer to live no longer for himself, but *for Him who died and rose again on his behalf*. Such is the core concept of *agapē*-love in the life of the Christian - everything is measured in view of our *union* with Christ's own person, death, and resurrection. Therefore, our love for Him is rooted in His matchless worth as the standard for our every affection and action in life.

We must also note, briefly, the breadth and application of the foremost commandment. In Mark 12:28-31, Christ's recitation of Deuteronomy 6:4-5 includes the additional word: *mind* [*dianoios*]. The inclusion of this word is understandable when

---

[63] 1 John 5:3: For this is the love of God, that we keep His commandments; and His commandments are not burdensome.

we consider the Hebraic understanding of the *heart* of man *[lebāb]*, which normally encompassed the idea of one's *mind and affections*. The Greeks tended to separate these components [heart and mind], whereas the Hebraic concept harmonized the two.[64] This observation is crucial since it reveals that the foremost commandment encompasses a full spectrum of affections, *thoughts, and convictions* within the worshipper, including: personal/relational knowledge [*yāḏă'*],[65] trust [*bēṭāḥ*],[66] delight ['*ānăḡ*],[67] devotion [*ḡôl*],[68] rest/dependence [*dāmăm*],[69] hope [*tôḥeleṯ*], filial fear/reverence [*yāre'*],[70] and joy [*semāḥôṯ*].[71] This is not an exhaustive list of godly thoughts and affections, but it offers a sample of the *ingredients*[72] of genuine love as found within God's Word.[73] What we must note in this summary is this: these

---

[64] *H. lebāb*: Heart, understanding, mind (also used in idioms such as "to set the heart upon" meaning "to think about" or "to want"). Harris, Theological Wordbook, 1:466.

[65] For some specific uses of *yāḏă'*, see Psalm 46:10, and 100:3. Also, in Psalm 37 David speaks of "God," not *generically*, but personally through his use of God's *personal memorial-name* [LORD ~ *yāhweh*]. David's frequent use of God's personal name reveals his *personal/relational knowledge* of the one true God who intimately loves His chosen people as His children.

[66] Psalm 37:3, 5.

[67] Psalm 37:4.

[68] Psalm 37:5.

[69] Psalm 37:7.

[70] Deuteronomy 10:12. "Filial affections are due to a father; love, reverence, delight in him, and fear to offend him, Romans viii. 15." Thomas Boston An illustration of the doctrines of the Christian religion with Respect to Faith and Practice upon the plan of the Assembly's Shorter Catechism: In Three Volumes (Printed by John Reid), p. 277.

[71] Psalm 16:11.

[72] Boston, An illustration of the doctrines of the Christian religion, p. 401.

[73] Matthew 22:40.

components of genuine love can only be understood in the context of a *relational union with God*, since the *relational concept of agapē* is central to everything thus described (contrary to the idea of *erōs*-love).[74] In addition, this harmonious expression of love is finally underscored with the concluding word: *strength [me'ôd]*, which denotes the fullness of devotion that God desires from His children.[75] This scalar adverb (strength/*me'ôd*) emphasizes a *full, thorough, and multifaceted* expression of love for God, rather than a partial or selective expression of one's thoughts and affections. Thus, every precious detail of the foremost commandment *ought* to

---

[74] More will be said about *erōs*-love in the next chapter (chapter 3), but the reader should understand that Lewis' influence here is significant. It was his belief that *agapē*-love could not be understood without *erōs*-love. As previously mentioned, Lewis admits that he tried to write his book by the standard of God's love (*via* the Apostle John's declaration that *God is love*), but then decided that this would be too difficult: "Every time I have tried to think the thing out along those lines I have ended in puzzles and contradictions. The reality is more complicated than I supposed." Then, following a quote from Plato, Lewis defers to his own personal experience, concluding that God's love must be understood *via* all the *root experiences* of human love: "'The highest...does not stand without the lowest.'" The honesty of his admission is telling, reminding the reader that the benchmark of his descriptions of love come, not from the source of all genuine love (God Himself), but from the subjective experiences and machinations of men. Lewis The Inspirational Writings of C.S. Lewis: *The Four Loves*, p. 213.

[75] *H. me'ôd*: This word, translated as "might" is a scalar adverb and serves the purpose emphasizing the magnitude of devotion from one's *heart and mind.* McBride observed: "The three parts of Deut 6:5: *lebāb* (heart), *nepeś* (soul or life), and *me'ôd* (muchness) rather than signifying different spheres of Biblical psychology seem to be semantically concentric. They were chosen to reinforce the absolute singularity of personal devotion to God. Thus *lebāb* denotes the intention or will of the whole man; *nepeś* means the whole self, a unity of flesh, will, and vitality; and *me'ôd* accents the superlative degree of total commitment to Yahweh." Harris, Theological Wordbook, 1:487.

be incorporated in our thinking whenever we talk about the Christian's expression of love for God, lest we degrade to the *art and thought of man.*[76]

The importance of this word for love, *agapē*, must not be underestimated.[77] Despite the secular and pagan notions of love found in the Graeco-Roman world, the biblical writers endeavored to define love, not by the naturalistic experiences of men, nor by their pagan mythologies, but by the transcendent reality of the *one true God - who is love (agapē).* Thus, exhaustive studies into the historical meaning and use of the word *agapē,* as defined by the secular world, cannot give us its fullest denotation and connotation. In fact, the word *agapē* supplied a *relatively* clean canvas for the biblical writers, especially since this word was the one least used in pre-biblical Greek, as noted in the *Theological Dictionary of the New Testament*:

> "...whereas *erōs* consistently engages the thinking of poets and philosophers from Homer to Plotinus, *agapan* hardly ever emerges as a subject of radical deliberation. It is indeed striking that the substantive *agapē* is almost completely lacking in pre-biblical Greek."[78]

---

[76] Consistent with his admission in the introduction of *The Four Loves,* Lewis frequently defers to his own experience as he attempts to develop a theology of love (e.g., "...if I may trust my own experience..."). Lewis, The Inspirational Writings of C.S. Lewis: *The Four Loves*, p. 287.

[77] This includes Deuteronomy 6:4-5 in the LXX: "...*kai agapēseis kurion ton theon sou...*"

[78] Gerhard Kittel, ed., Theological Dictionary of the New Testament, (Grand Rapids, Michigan: WM. B. Eerdmans Publishing Company, 1991), 1:37.

A.T. Robertson comments on this matter as well, first citing James Moffatt as follows:

> "'When Christianity first began to think and speak in Greek, it took up *agapē* and its group of terms more freely, investing them with the new glow with which the N.T. writings make us familiar, a content which is invariably religious' (Moffatt, *Love in the New Testament*, p. 40). The New Testament never uses the word *erōs* (lust)." [79]

Of all the terms that might have been used to convey the Hebraic concept of God's love (H. *'āhāḇ*), *agapē* was employed within the LXX, and continued in the New Testament, as the principal term for this central affection in genuine worship. What is crucial in all this is as follows: the love *of God* within the child of God is not a new and improved version of human love; nor is it a slight modification of natural affections. Instead, it is the product of the spiritual and miraculous transformation called *new birth* or *regeneration*.[80] Thus, this love *of God* is the greatest love of all. What we learned from the Apostle John, in 1 John 4:7-8, is that *"...love [agapē] is from God...the one who does not love [agapōn] does not know God."* John's point is extremely important and profound: God's love is an *alien affection* such that it is impossible to know such love by personal experience

---

[79] A.T. Robertson, <u>Word Pictures in the New Testament</u> (Baker Book House, Grand Rapids, Michigan, 1931) Vol.V, <u>First Thessalonians - Chapter I</u>, pp. 8-9.

[80] 2 Corinthians 5:17: Therefore if anyone is in Christ, he is a new creature; the old things passed away; behold, new things have come. Galatians 2:20: "I have been crucified with Christ; and it is no longer I who live, but Christ lives in me; and the life which I now live in the flesh I live by faith in the Son of God, who loved me and gave Himself up for me. Romans 5:5: and hope does not disappoint, because the love of God has been poured out within our hearts through the Holy Spirit who was given to us.

or effort. Ultimately, the natural man cannot know such an alien love *by his fallen nature*. If the sinner is to experience this transcendent love from God, then he must be born *from God above*:

> John 3:3: Jesus answered and said to him, "Truly, truly, I say to you, unless one is born again he cannot see the kingdom of God."

This familiar expression, *born again (genēthē anothen)*, could be translated as: *born from above (anothen)*. I would suggest that the latter expression should be preferred as supplying the root idea in the Savior's teaching. Men do not know God because, apart from a miracle of grace *from above*, He is unknowable in any salvific sense. Thus, His divine love is equally unknowable apart from such spiritual regeneration *from above*. While this may seem to be too simple a notion to merit the time and attention, the reader should be aware that such thinking has fallen on hard times in recent years. What has become fashionable is the belief that God can be known through an emphasis on the natural affections of fallen men. Such was the view of Lewis who argued that *the highest [love] does not stand without the lowest*.[81] While such a view may seem interesting and fascinating to some, it is a direct contradiction to John's teaching in 1 John 4:7-10. Those who do not know God cannot know His love. Such men may wax eloquent on their religious passions and affections all day long, but without the true love of God, their proud rantings are in vain. All that is being established in this section is the reality that God's love is unique, and that such love is singled out as the foremost affection in all genuine worship:

---

[81] Lewis, The Inspirational Writings of C.S. Lewis: *The Four Loves*, p. 214.

- **It is the basis of our redemption:** Ephesians 2:4, 1 John 4:7-10, John 3:16-18.

- **It is the first-fruit of the Spirit:** Galatians 5:22-23: 22. But the fruit of the Spirit is love, joy, peace, patience, kindness, goodness, faithfulness, 23. gentleness, self-control; against such things there is no law.

- **It is the principal expression of genuine worship:** Mark 12:28-31, John 14:31.[82]

- **Without it we are nothing, and can do nothing for His ultimate glory:** 1 Corinthians 13, John 5:39-47, Ephesians 3:14-21.

But we cannot stop here, for the centrality of such love extends to every facet of Christian life:

- **It is the bedrock of every godly marriage and family:** Ephesians 5:1-6:4 & Titus 2:3-5.

- **It is the mandate of Christian fellowship:** 1 John 3:1-13.

- **It is the motive of our Christian witness and outreach:** Ephesians 5:1-17, Matthew 5:43-48

---

[82] The greatest fulfillment of the foremost commandment (Deuteronomy 6:4-5) is Christ Himself who desired that the whole world would see and know of His love for the Father - *John 14:31: but so that the world may know that I love the Father, I do exactly as the Father commanded Me. Get up, let us go from here.*

CHAPTER 2 - THE GREATEST LOVE OF ALL

Few words have such centrality in the Bible as does *agapē*. Though this word was nearly neglected in the secular culture, it was taken over and used by the biblical writers to describe something that no man could ever discover by natural means. Such love, as defined by God's messengers, is something that is embraced in faith by all genuine believers:

> 1 John 4:16: We have come to know and have believed the love which God has for us. God is love, and the one who abides in love abides in God, and God abides in him.

In closing, I would ask that the reader consider the profundity of 1 John 4:16 - *it is quite a statement!* John is highlighting for us a special, transcendent love: *the love which God has for us.* If you are a believer at all, you "have believed the love [*agapēn*] which God has for us." John is helping us to understand that the genuine children of God believe in the *true God*, as defined by His *true love* rather than any counterfeit - *and there are many counterfeits.* The Greek world was filled with such counterfeit forms of love, but the love of the true God is utterly *incomparable.* When we consider the size and magnitude of such a term as *agapē*-love, it should be evident that even the slightest manipulation of its meaning or centrality could produce a massive upheaval of truth. No element of Scripture should ever be maligned or twisted, but such a principle is only strengthened when considering the centrality of such doctrines as the love of God. Sadly, in the modern day, there is a great deal of tweaking going on in the name of theological novelty - and much of it is impacting this crucial and central subject. As well, though their systems of thought may seem new, they are not. Throughout history men have made the grave mistake of infusing extrabiblical thinking within their interpretation of biblical texts, and the transitive propagation of such error is often vast. There are various ways in which men have infused false forms of thinking into the subject of God's love - I will not be able to address them all here - however, it may suffice to say that any deviation from *biblical love* will ultimately produce a *man-centered* corruption of some form or another. Thus, *Scriptural definitions* of God's love and freedom must rule over every other notion of human love and freedom, *for God is the standard and benchmark of everything.* Should we reverse that order of evaluation, we will produce a useless, man-centered theology. This is true for both the Arminian and Reformed communities. I fear that this truth is too easily ignored, and supplies an unseen danger to those who might be tempted to presume absolute immunity from such man-centeredness. It doesn't matter who is propagating a false understanding of the subject of love: if they are exalting the art and thought of man, then they are not magnifying God's true nature and glory - *period*. In the next chapter, we will examine the nature of God's love *with even greater detail*, considering the historic manner in which this subject has been corrupted by man-centered philosophies - *just as we face in the modern day.* By this we will consider the crucial nature of Christian affections, considering the great danger that comes when men obfuscate the clear teaching of Scripture. The biblical writers, under the leading of the Holy Spirit, have supplied us with several key details about the uniqueness and beauty of God's love, in contrast to the counterfeits of this world. Let us then proceed with submissive hearts[83] and further examine this essential subject.

---

[83] Isaiah 66:2: "For My hand made all these things, thus all these things came into being," declares the Lord. "But to this one I will look, to him who is humble and contrite of spirit, and who trembles at My word."

CHAPTER 3
THE AFFECTIONS
OF LOVE

> *"Where a true Eros is present resistance to his commands feels like apostasy."*[84]
> *- C.S. Lewis, The Four Loves*

As already mentioned, the modern world is not much different from the ancient one. Just as the Athenians worshipped *an unknown god,* so too do many today. As we contemplate how this impacts contemporary notions of love, we must remember that every generation of mankind is, by nature, hopelessly stuck in the mud of human pride, selfishness, and relational indifference. In all of this, we can confess with Solomon that there really is nothing new under the sun. Our only hope of being freed from such repetitious sin is through the power of God's Word. Without God's revelation, we are left with our own vain imaginations. As this relates to our discussion of the love of God, the reader should know that within the last century there has been a resurgence in the acceptance of the ancient concepts surrounding *erōs*-love within modern Evangelicalism. As well, Roman Catholicism has carried the torch of such thinking for centuries. This was recently reaffirmed by Pope Benedict XVI in his papal encyclical on love:

> "In philosophical and theological debate, these distinctions have often been radicalized to the point of establishing a clear antithesis between them...Yet *eros* and *agape* - ascending love and descending love - can never be completely separated."[85]

Among Evangelicals, the infusion of *erōs* into the scriptural definitions of *agapē*-love is greatly attributable to the writings

---

[84] Lewis The Inspirational Writings of C.S. Lewis: *The Four Loves*, p. 273.
[85] Pope Benedict XVI, Deus Caritas Est (Encyclical Letter, December 25th 2005).

of C.S. Lewis. His popularity has done much to reinvigorate this concept of *erōs-love* in contemporary literature, producing an abundance of confusion regarding the foremost commandment. His influence continues to span the Evangelical and Catholic world.[86] The hidden danger of Lewis' writings is that his views on love are deeply subjective, leading to several defective notions of worship and human freedom. As already mentioned, Rob Bell's book, *Love Wins*, has re-exposed such defections. However, as we learned in the previous chapter, it is God who is ultimately free in the direction and application of His redemptive love, and the recipients of such love (His redeemed children) are now free within the *infinite constraint* of Christ's eternal love. Such a *constraint* is *genuine freedom* and runs entirely against Bell's faulty presentation of love and human freedom. This is why we initiated our discussion of love, not through an analysis of human affections, but by the standard of God's love through the foremost commandment. Our examination of this commandment was crucial, for it reminds us of the Lord's desire for genuine devotion rather than superficial duty.[87] Satan knows very well what is dear to the heart of God, and for this reason I am persuaded that the demons have a great hatred for the doctrine of godly love. It therefore behooves us to guard this doctrine, like any other, with great care and concern. I might even suggest that as it is

---

[86] "The conviction of the usefulness of *The Four Loves* toward an understanding of the psychology and value of love has grown steadily among the leaders of different Christian churches. Thus for some years quotations from it have been appearing in the sermons and addresses of Pope John Paul II." Sayer, Jack, A Life of C.S. Lewis, p. 390.

[87] Hosea 6:6 For I delight in loyalty rather than sacrifice, And in the knowledge of God rather than burnt offerings.

central to the *foremost* commandment; our guardianship of it should be delivered with *foremost zeal.*

The great danger that we must now address is the manner in which the doctrine of love is being compromised through the infusion of secular philosophy. As we now consider the subject of the *affections of love* in this chapter, we must go beyond Lewis' particular influence on Rob Bell. In fact, I would argue that there are *many writers* of the present day who are producing dangerous conflations of *agapē* and *erōs*-love because of Lewis' influence. In his book, *The Four Loves,* Lewis' chapter on *erōs*-love leads the reader to believe that there is a legitimate expression of such love in the Christian's life, even assigning the same affection to Christ Himself:

> "...Christ said to us through *Erōs*, 'Thus – just like this – with this prodigality – not counting the cost – you are to love me and the least of my brethren."[88]

Lewis' treatment of the four loves (*erōs, philōs, philostorgē, agapē*) lacks the needful grounding of the Scriptures, and thus, he wanders through a forest of his own thoughts, erroneously incorporating false constructs regarding *erōs*-love throughout his journey. The result is that the reader is led to believe that *erōs*-love, with some modifications, has a proper place in the Christian life. Lewis' emphasis on personal passion and desire takes him to some very dark forms of reasoning. For example, when describing his experiences at Wynyard Boarding School ("Wyvern"), he expresses his toleration for pederasty, as a

---

[88] Lewis The Inspirational Writings of C.S. Lewis: *The Four Loves*, p. 272.

source of "certain good things," while opining about the oasis found within a forbidden *erōs*:

> "If those of us who have known a school like Wyvern dared to speak the truth, we should have to say that pederasty, however great an evil in itself, was, in that time and place, the only foothold or cranny left for certain good things. It was the only counterpoise to the social struggle; the one oasis (though green only with weeds and moist only with fetid water) in the burning desert of competitive ambition. In his unnatural love affairs, and perhaps only there, the Blood went a little out of himself, forgot for a few hours that he was One of the Most important People There Are. It softens the picture. A perversion was the only chink left through which something spontaneous and uncalculating could creep in. Plato was right after all. Eros, turned upside down, blackened, distorted, and filthy, still bore the traces of his divinity."[89]

But Lewis' philosophical relativism isn't the only source of his defective views regarding love. More fundamentally, Lewis offers several groundless definitions of *erōs*–love, conflating the ideas of *agapē*-love with *erōs* and doing so without a single shred of biblical evidence. Thus, when attempting to describe the nature of *erōs*-love, he fallaciously makes *erōs*-love sound very much like *agapē*-love:

> "In some mysterious but quite indisputable fashion the lover desires the Beloved herself, not the pleasure she can give."[90]

What is lacking in Lewis' *The Four Loves* is a serious understanding of the historical significance of the Greek term

---

[89] Ibid., *Surprised by Joy*, p. 61.

[90] Ibid., *The Four Loves*, p. 264.

erōs, not just as an expression of human desire, but especially as a part of the mythology involving the god *Erōs*, along with his spirit-progeny: *hedonē*. The absence of this biblical/historical background yields massive confusion within Lewis, and those who consume and promote his literature tend to repeat such confusion. Those who frequently appeal to Lewis' writings often argue that *agapē* and *erōs* are not at all distinct, but actually converge as one essence of love.[91] Thinking such as this reveals a deeply troubling presumption.[92] But do the Scriptures reveal the thought of the Lord being a God of *erōs*-love? Is this idea defensible?

I must argue that it is not.

The one monumental fact about *erōs*-love, that Lewis missed or ignored, is that the Spirit-led writers of the New Testament *avoided this word entirely*. This is no small problem for the

---

[91] "Historically, ethicists have tended to distinguish these two forms of love as *agapē* and *erōs*, or benevolence, and complacency. Not only is there no linguistic basis for such a distinction, but conceptually both resolve into one kind of love at the root. God's *agapē* does not 'transcend' his *erōs*, but expresses it." John Piper, <u>Desiring God: Meditations of a Christian Hedonist</u>, (Colorado Springs, CO: Multnomah Books, 2011), p. 124n.

[92] In his papal encyclical, Pope Benedict labors at length in order to retain the use of *erōs*-love. Consistent with his tradition, he employs the notion of a synergism of the old and the new man (*erōs* and *agapē*), as opposed to the biblical presentation of a monergistic/radical transformation of death unto life (Romans 6:1-11) such that God's *agapē* replaces the *erōs* of fallen man: "Even if *eros* is at first mainly covetous and ascending, a fascination for the great promise of happiness of the other, is concerned more and more with the beloved, bestows itself and wants to 'be there for' the other. The element of *agape* thus enters into this love, for otherwise *eros* is impoverished and even loses its own nature." Pope Benedict XVI, <u>Deus Caritas Est</u> (Encyclical Letter, December 25th 2005).

proponents of *erōs*-love, especially since the concept of *erōs* was the most popular one in the 1st century Graeco-Roman world, being the highest expression of love *par excellence*. Thus, one cannot argue that this word's omission was the product of general ignorance or forgetfulness. The New Testament's rejection of this term is, I believe, *self-evident*. When one considers the core philosophy of this term, it should be clear to the reader as to why it is that *erōs* was so thoroughly avoided in the N.T. In the most primitive analysis of things, what Christ brought to mankind was something that transcended the self-centered orientation of *erōs*. I must restate the fact that *erōs* was more than a philosophy of self-pleasure, it was the formal name of the god of love, whose spiritual progeny, *hedonē*, embodied a similar notion of autonomous self-delight. In this section, we will examine why it is that these words were so deeply problematic, and consider the danger that Lewis has posed through the reinsertion of such language and concepts:

1. The Gospel transcends all human philosophies: The Graeco-Roman world was filled with the ether of Greek *philosophy* and mythology.[93] Consequently, the Greek *language* was thoroughly embedded in this same ether, increasing the difficulty of communicating the incomparable message of the Gospel. But the Apostolic commitment was quite clear. When communicating the transcendent truths of the Gospel to the Greek world, the Apostles

---

[93] "While gods and goddesses resided in every temple and could be seen in secular surroundings, too, at street corners or ensconced in niches in the town hall, nevertheless it was not the stone population inside sanctuary circuits but outside temples themselves that contributed most to the total of 30,000 statues of deities estimated to exist in the Empire as a whole; and this population received additions all the time, to the point of needing to be thinned out." Ramsay MacMullen, Paganism in the Roman Empire (Yale University Press, New Haven and London, 1981), p. 31.

endeavored to do so *without the art, thought, and reasoning of mere men*. Thus, the Apostolic mission included the process of tearing down all extra-biblical thinking that was raised up against the knowledge of God:

> 2 Corinthians 10:4-5: 4. for the weapons of our warfare are not of the flesh, but divinely powerful for the destruction of fortresses. 5. We are destroying speculations and every lofty thing raised up against the knowledge of God, and we are taking every thought captive to the obedience of Christ...

The *fortresses* of which Paul speaks consisted of the *speculations* and *lofty thoughts* raised up against the knowledge of God. This battle strategy stands in tandem with Paul's instruction to the Athenians: *the Divine Nature is not...an image formed by the art and thought of man (Acts 17:29, as previously addressed)*. This labor of distinguishing Gospel truth is crucial. Thus, when Paul and Barnabas were mistaken as Hermes and Zeus, by the natives of Lystra, their response wasn't to adorn costumes of their respective and mistaken identities as a means of communicating truth about the Lord - *such a strategy would have polluted their message.* Instead, they tore their robes in utter grief over the people's idolatry, and made a solemn Gospel-appeal beginning with Psalm 146:6. In other words, they never accommodated the culture; instead, they confronted it with the transcendent truth of God's Word. The entire religious culture of the Graeco-Roman world was a stumbling block to the Gospel, and Paul feared that men would be drawn away by such worldly mythology.[94] Therefore, it is no surprise that when Paul was in Athens, his spirit was "provoked" upon seeing a *city full of idols.* These known idols could not be used as instrumental props for preaching Christ. Exactly how could Paul communicate Christ by using the images of *Zeus, Hermes, Eros, or Hedone* as preaching aids?

---

[94] 2 Timothy 4:4 ...and will turn away their ears from the truth and will turn aside to myths (*muthos*).

As a messenger of the Gospel, he couldn't. These idols were a disgusting provocation to any messenger of the Gospel in view of their ideology of selfishness and rank idolatry. However, as previously observed, Paul did use one prop, and it was the only *tabula rasa* within view: *the altar to an unknown god*. The banality of this object is what made it useful. It supplied no image or knowledge of a supposed deity, but stood as a bare acknowledgement of the Athenian's ignorance of the one true God. This is a precious example for us, as Paul pierced through the fog of Greek mythology and disclosed that which his audience needed to hear *without any mythological pollution*.

2. Not all Greek words are created equal: In view of the Apostolic example before us, we should keep in mind just how thoughtful they were when dealing with a culture steeped in idolatry. Such thoughtfulness extended to their choice and use of words. Admittedly, Paul's use of the *altar to an unknown god* seems simple enough, but it gets a bit more difficult when it comes to Greek words and their meanings. As a principle, we can readily admit that the aura of Greek and Roman mythology influenced the Greek language as a whole, but such influence varied from word to word. Such is the case for the words for love. Very simply, the word *agapē* did not carry much philosophical baggage, which, like the *altar to an unknown god*, made it all the more useful under the guidance of the N.T. writers, as previously noted:

> "It is indeed striking that the substantive *agapē* is almost completely lacking in pre-biblical Greek."[95]

However, what denotative and connotative history *agapē* did have served as an important base of meaning, especially in view of its important emphasis of honoring others in the context of a relationship:

---

[95]Kittel, Theological Dictionary, 1:37.

> "*agapaō*, originally meaning to honour or welcome, is in classical Gk. the least specifically defined word; it is frequently used synonymously with *phileō* without any necessarily strict distinction in meaning. In the NT, however, *agapaō* and the noun *agapē* have taken on a particular significance in that they are used to speak of the love of God or the way of life based on it." [96]

The Septuagint stands as a forerunner to the elevation of *agapē*, teaching us, by contrast, much about the historic understanding of *erōs*, as philologist Richard Trench observed in his work - *Synonyms of the New Testament*:

> "I observe in conclusion that *erōs, eran, erastes,* never occur in the N.T., but the two latter occasionally in the Septuagint; thus *eran*, Esth. 2:17; Prov. 4:6; *erastes* generally in a dishonorable sense as 'paramour' (Ezek. 16:33; Hos. 2:5); yet once or twice (as Wisd. 8:2) more honorably, not as='amasius,' but 'amator.' Their absence is significant. It is in part no doubt to be explained from the fact that, by the corrupt use of the world, they had become so steeped in sensual passion, carried such an atmosphere of unholiness about them (see Origen, *Prol. in Cant. Opp.* tom iii. pp. 28–30), that the truth of God abstained from the defiling contact with them; yea, devised a new word rather than betake itself to one of these."[97]

The writers of the Septuagint associated the Hebrew word *'āhăb* with the Greek word *agapē*. Only three references in the LXX employ the word *erōs*, each denoting the thought of depraved

---

[96] Colin Brown Ed., The New International Dictionary of New Testament Theology, (Zondervan Publishing House, Grand Rapids MI, 1986), 2:538-539.
[97] Trench, R. C. (2003). *Synonyms of the New Testament.* (9th ed., improved.) (43). Bellingham, WA: Logos Research Systems, Inc.

affections or barrenness.[98] In short, the LXX translators avoided the term entirely, as an expression of *godly love*, and employed the terms *philos* and *agapē* instead. This use of *philos* and *agapē* continued on in the N.T. but with no mention of *erōs* at all, and the only related term, *hēdonē*, is used five times to speak of lust, similar to the concept of *erōs*.[99]

As in their mythological genealogy, the words *erōs* and *hēdonē* bore some family likeness in meaning, though *erōs* was much more popular and well-defined. The Greek ideal in life was utterly grounded in the pursuit of autonomous self-satisfaction as the highest goal and achievement of any individual. This pursuit of self-pleasure involved the instrumentality of various things and people, but at the heart of it all was *self-gratification*. This is even true regarding the sacrifices offered to the gods, whether sexual or not. All sacrifices were believed to be necessary for the strengthening of the gods, *but for the ultimate good of man*:

> "The gods were essentially gods of activity-they did things, such as controlling childbirth or repelling disease-and activity requires

---

[98] Proverbs 7:18; 30:16, Psalm 35:11 (LXX: 34:11).

[99] Titus 3:3: For we also once were foolish ourselves, disobedient, deceived, enslaved to various lusts (*hēdonais*) and pleasures, spending our life in malice and envy, hateful, hating one another. James 4:1, 3: 1. What is the source of quarrels and conflicts among you? Is not the source your pleasures (*hēdonēn*) that wage war in your members?, ...3. You ask and do not receive, because you ask with wrong motives, so that you may spend it on your pleasures. Luke 8:14: The seed which fell among the thorns, these are the ones who have heard, and as they go on their way they are choked with worries and riches and pleasures (*hēdonōn*) of this life, and bring no fruit to maturity. 2 Peter 2:13: suffering wrong as the wages of doing wrong. They count it a pleasure (*hēdonēn*) to revel in the daytime. They are stains and blemishes, reveling in their deceptions, as they carouse with you.

vitality. If the god's vitality was not sustained and renewed, that activity would be weakened and they would no longer be able to function efficiently. Crops would fail or disease would spread because the relevant gods did not have enough vigour to perform their tasks even if they wanted to."[100]

"...The existence of the gods depends to an appreciable extent on man's devotion to them. Varro puts this quite simply when he writes: 'I am afraid that some gods may perish simply from neglect.'"[101]

This very form of thinking was confronted by the Apostle Paul when he preached in Athens:

Acts 17:24-25: 24. "The God who made the world and all things in it, since He is Lord of heaven and earth, does not dwell in temples made with hands; 25. nor is He served by human hands, as though He needed anything, since He Himself gives to all people life and breath and all things;"

The religious belief system that was embedded within *erōs* revealed the worshipper's ultimate commitment, not to the gods, *but to self.* Thus, all devotion to the gods was seen as *essential for their subsistence,* but for the ultimate benefit of mankind. The supposed worthiness of such deities became secondary within this scheme of thinking. It is this man-centeredness that defined the very essence of *erōs*: *the gods existed for the good-pleasure of man.* Sexual and animal sacrifices were not seen as optional, but absolutely essential to

---

[100] Robert Maxwell Ogilvie, The Romans and Their Gods (WW Norton & Company, New York, 1969), p. 42.
[101] Ibid.

support the gods *for the good of mankind*. Additionally, personal ecstasy was believed to enhance the sacrifices offered, which ultimately resulted in a greater beneficence *towards man*.[102]

Indeed, everything was a cycle of self.

Thus, the lack of Christian participation in such sacrifices is what led others to believe that the followers of Christ were the hostile source of all calamities. Society's disdain for such non-participation continued to increase with time:

> Minucius Felis: "You apprehensive and anxiety-ridden Christians abstain from innocent pleasures. You don't watch the public spectacles, you don't take part in the processions, you absent yourselves from the public banquets, you shrink away from sacred games, sacrificial meat, and altar libations. That's how frightened you are of the gods whose existence you deny!"[103]

In a hedonistic environment such as the 1st century Graeco-Roman world, it is no wonder that the Christian community had difficulty participating in the annual festivals of the Roman Empire. Such *antisocial* conduct provoked the earliest persecutions:

> Tacitus: "Nero had self-acknowledged Christians arrested. Then, on their information, large numbers of others were condemned - not so much for incendiarism as for their *anti-social tendencies*. Their deaths were made farcical. Dressed in wild animals' skins, they were

---

[102] Brown, ed., The New International Dictionary of New Testament Theology, 2:536.

[103] Minucius Felix, *Octavius* 8.4, 5; 9.2, 4-7; 10.2, 5; 12:5.

torn to pieces by dogs, or crucified, or made into torches to be ignited after dark as substitutes for daylight."[104]

The Greek concept of *erōs*-love in worship was deeply self-oriented and the worshipping community carefully protected its place within the culture. We could easily say that the contemporary version of this is the religion of *self-esteem*. By contrast, the Christian reality of love had a radically different orientation, making the *root* expressions *erōs* and *hēdonē* impossible to use in any godly sense. As noted in the prior section, the true love of God is centered in the idea of *union with another (i.e., a relationship)*. For the Christian, such a union is revealed in the foremost commandment such that true worshippers can call the Lord *their God* in view of His initiation of a freely sovereign, redeeming love (Mark 12:28-31, Deuteronomy 6:4-5; 7:7-8). Overall, the defining element in *agapē*-love is union with Christ, as previously noted:

> 1 John 4:7-10: 7. Beloved, let us love one another, for love is from God; and everyone who loves is born of God and knows God. 8. The one who does not love does not know God, for God is love. 9. By this the love of God was manifested in us, that God has sent His only begotten Son into the world so that we might live through Him. 10. In this is love, not that we loved God, but that He loved us and sent His Son to be the propitiation for our sins.

This union with God in Christ establishes the very core and distinction of *agapē*. Unlike *erōs*, the affections of the Christian are always centered in a *relationship* with the One who elects and redeems His own out of His *free and sovereign love*.

---

[104] Tacitus, The Annals of Imperial Rome (Barnes & Noble Books, New York, 1993), p. 365, italics mine.

Therefore, Christian love is always grounded in a Christ-centered valuation of everything, including our relationships with a spouse, children, other brethren, and the lost of this world. In this sense, the pre-biblical notion of *agapē* (honoring others) is somewhat preserved in the N.T.:

> "The translators probably preferred the words of the *agapaō* group which convey less affective emphasis since they designate 'a sober kind of love—love in the sense of placing a high value upon some person or thing, or of receiving them with favour' (Warnach, *SacVB* 518; in this connection see also Joly)."[105]

Such a concept of honor within *agapē*-love reveals a beautiful expression of harmony between the O.T. and the N.T.: children are taught to honor (*appreciate* or highly esteem) their father and mother in the fifth commandment (Exodus 20:12, Ephesians 6:2) as their earliest pedagogy of filial love and devotion. Such are the early *tutorials* that point us to the higher calling of being the children of God. In view of this, it is not difficult to see the strength and centrality of the term *agapē*. By significant contrast, at the core of *erōs* one will not find such a concept of *otherness* because individual passion remains supreme. It is this self-centered pursuit of pleasure that saturated the culture, and it influenced every aspect of life:

> "What the Greek seeks in *eros* is intoxication, and this is to him religion. To be sure, reflection is the finest of the flirts which the heavenly powers have set in the heart of man (Soph. Ant., 683 ff.); it is the fulfillment of humanity in measure. More glorious, however, is

---

[105]Balz, H. R., & Schneider, G. (1990-c1993). *Exegetical dictionary of the New Testament*. Translation of: Exegetisches Worterbuch zum Neuen Testament. (1:9). Grand Rapids, Mich.: Eerdmans.

the *eros* which puts an end to all reflection, which sets all the senses in a frenzy, which bursts the measure and form of all humanistic humanity and lifts man above himself...It is a god, and he is powerful even above the gods: *turannos theon te kanthropon* (Eur. Fr., 132, Nauck). All the forces of heaven and earth are forces of second rank compared with the one and only supreme power of *eros*. No choice is left, nor will, nor freedom, to the man who is seized by its tyrannical omnipotence, and he finds supreme bliss in being mastered by it."[106]

"*Eran* is passionate love which desires the other for itself...*Erōs* seeks in others the fulfillment of its own life's hunger. *Agapan* must often be translated "to show love"; it is a giving, active love on the other's behalf."[107]

The most frequent application of this self-ecstasy (*erōs*) was found in sensual delight, from the worship of the gods, to the institution of marriage. The common fruit of such *erōs*-love was *personal ecstasy* at the greater expense of *relational intimacy*, respectively:

Hymenaeus' wedding poem: "Live well, newlyweds, and spend your youth in constant lovemaking."[108]

"Marriage, which had once been a lifelong economic union, was now among a hundred thousand Romans a passing adventure of no great spiritual significance, a loose contract for the mutual provision of physiological conveniences or political aid."[109]

---

[106] Kittel, Theological Dictionary, 1:35.

[107] Ibid., p. 37.

[108] Hymenaeus' wedding poem: Jo-Ann Shelton, As The Romans Did, A Source Book in Roman Social History (Oxford University Press, New York, 1988), p. 43.

[109] Will Durant, The Story of Civilization, (Simon and Schuster, NY, 1963), 3:363.

Sadly, such selfishness and relational indifference is very much here with us today! Yet this frenzy of self-satisfaction was not limited to sexual pleasure, but encompassed every form of desire. Even food was utilized, beyond its design, for the sake of such self-satisfaction:

> "Custom allowed the diner to empty his stomach with an emetic after a heavy banquet. Some gluttons performed this operation during the meal and then returned to appease their hunger; *vomunt ut edant, edunt ut vomant,* said Senecca - 'they vomit to eat, and eat to vomit.'" (Seneca *Ad Helviam*, x, 3)[110]

Here again, we see that what is distinct in the notion of *erōs* is this strict *self-orientation.* Contrary to the biblical notions of love, which are always predicated upon the concept of union with another, *erōs*-love has one central commitment – *self* – and this was no ancillary concept or thought. This idea was rehearsed and celebrated in the religious festivals that often included pursuits of drunken and sexual pleasures, with 175 such festivals honored by the year 354 AD.[111]

Without these concepts in hand, we may be tempted to accept Lewis' proposition that *erōs* has some redeemable qualities in a

---

[110] Ibid., 3:377.

[111] Having many gods to worship, and many provinces to milk, Rome had many holidays, once solemn with religious pageantry, now gay with secular delight. In the early Empire there were in the Roman year seventy-six festival days on which *ludi* were performed. Of these, fifty-five were *ludi scenici,* devoted to plays or mimes; twenty-two were games in the circus, the stadium, or the amphitheater. The number of the *ludi* increased until by A.D. 354 they were presented on 175 days in the year (Suetonius, "Vespasian," 19). Ibid., 3:377-378.

Christian context. The danger of this view should be obvious, especially when we consider how the Corinthian church was exhibiting a similar misunderstanding in their day. The secularizing influence of *erōs* in their worship is evident in the Apostle's rebuke of their:

- Divisions through personal followings (1 Cor. 1).

- Selfish lawsuits against one another (1 Cor. 6).

- Their toleration of sexual sin (1 Cor. 5-6).

- Their drunken debauchery and abuse of the Lord's table (1 Cor. 11).

- Their self-styled worship and loveless contortion of spiritual gifts (1 Cor. 12-14).

- Their dangerous rejection of Apostolic authority (1 Cor. 4).

Thus, Paul's central discourse on *agapē-love* in 1 Corinthians 13 is crucial. He reminds them of the distinctive nature of such love in contrast to pagan counterfeits. Every quality of love mentioned in 1 Corinthians 13 can only be understood in view of the believer's *relational union with Christ*:

- "...Love is patient, love is kind..." (because we endure[112] and give[113] for Christ's sake).

---

[112] Galatians 6:1-2: 1. Brethren, even if anyone is caught in any trespass, you who are spiritual, restore such a one in a spirit of gentleness; each one looking to

- "[love]...is not jealous; love does not brag and is not arrogant..." (because Christ deserves the glory, not we ourselves[114]).

- "[love]...does not act unbecomingly..." (because the love of Christ controls us[115]).

- "[love]...does not seek its own..." (*because the love of Christ controls us* and we no longer live for ourselves, but for Him who died and rose again on our behalf[116]).

- "[love]...is not provoked, does not take into account a wrong suffered..." (because Christ is the coming King and Judge of all[117]).

- "[love]...does not rejoice in unrighteousness, but rejoices with the truth..." (because Christ is the way and the truth and the life[118]).

---

yourself, so that you too will not be tempted. 2. Bear one another's burdens, and thereby fulfill the law of Christ..

[113] Ephesians 4:32: Be kind to one another, tender-hearted, forgiving each other, just as God in Christ also has forgiven you..

[114] 1 Corinthians 1:30-31: 30. But by His doing you are in Christ Jesus, who became to us wisdom from God, and righteousness and sanctification, and redemption, 31. so that, just as it is written, "Let him who boasts, boast in the Lord.".

[115] 2 Corinthians 5:14: For the love of Christ controls us, having concluded this, that one died for all, therefore all died;.

[116] 2 Corinthians 5:15: and He died for all, so that they who live might no longer live for themselves, but for Him who died and rose again on their behalf..

[117] Acts 17:31: "...because He has fixed a day in which He will judge the world in righteousness through a Man whom He has appointed, having furnished proof to all men by raising Him from the dead."

- "[love]...bears all things, believes all things, hopes all things, endures all things..." (because Christ is our reason for living, our surety, and the object of our faith and hope).

Without the thought of union with Christ, such definitions of love have no meaning whatsoever. Such love is supernaturally rooted in Him and could never be derived from human nature alone. Contextually speaking, we should also note that when Paul declares: *"love (agapē) does not seek its own,"* he is reminding his audience that their selfishness must never be confused with genuine godly affections. The prevalence of temple prostitution in Corinth was massive,[119] and the culture thought nothing of seeking out their own pleasures, in worship, in the ecstasy of *erōs*. Such prevailing temptations were common in light of the broader realities of their day:

> "... *erōs* is love which desires to have or take possession. The vb. *eraō* and the noun *erōs*, on the other hand, denote the love between man and woman which embraces longing, craving and desire. The Greek's delight in bodily beauty and sensual desires found expression here in the Dionysiac[120] approach to, and feeling for, life. Sensual ecstasy leaves moderation and proportion far behind, and the Gk. tragedians (e.g. Soph., *Ant.* 781 ff.) knew the irresistible

---

[118] John 14:6: Jesus said to him, "I am the way, and the truth, and the life; no one comes to the Father but through Me."

[119] 1 Corinthians 6:15-20.

[120] Dionysus was the god of the grape harvest, and in the later Roman era, the tradition of Bacchus supplied a correlative mythology. The combined force of these mythologies is seen in the well formulated tradition of the Bacchanalia, celebrated in orgiastic festivals, accompanied with wine, music, dance, and ecstatic expressions of worship. Robert Turcan, <u>The Cults of the Roman Empire</u>, (Blackwell Publishers, Oxford UK, 1996), pp., 291-293.

power of *Erōs* - the god of love bore the same name - which forgot all reason, will and discretion on the way to ecstasy. There was also a more mystical understanding of *erōs*, whereby the Greeks sought to reach and go beyond normal human limitations in order to attain perfection. As well as the fertility cults with their oriental influences, and their glorification of the generating *Erōs* in nature, there were the mystery religions, whose rites were intended to unite the participant with the godhead."[121]

These fallen affections of mankind reveal a stark contrast to the love that is of God. In contrast to mankind's selfish inventions, we find that the ultimate template of godly love is wonderfully revealed in the *relational affection found within the Trinity*, as expressed in the words: *agapē* and *philos*.[122] The tainted nature of the term *erōs* should be self-evident. Its connection to the idolatry of *Erōs/hēdonē*, coupled with its self-seeking focus, made it a word that was useless for any godly purposes. Such a subjective focus on self-satisfaction was antithetical to the more *relational* ideal set forth by the N.T. writers. Even the second component of the foremost commandment is predicated on *agapē* love (*you shall love [agapēseis] your neighbor as yourself*), since the children of God do not *subsist autonomously*, but as those who have been *bought with a price*:

> 1 Corinthians 6:19-20: 19. Or do you not know that your body is a temple of the Holy Spirit who is in you, whom you have from God, and that you are not your own? 20. For you have been bought with a price: therefore glorify God in your body.

---

[121] Brown, The New International Dictionary of New Testament Theology, 2:538.

[122] Isaiah 5:1-2, Ephesians 1:6, John 5:20, 10:17, 14:31, 17:24.

Thus, the believer's self-care/love is now rooted in the love of Christ, rather than the lusts of the flesh.[123] The battle of the biblical writers was to reveal, not only the *unknown God* to their world, but also the *unknown affections* which the Graeco-Roman world did not understand, *nor could they understand apart from divine grace and revelation.* It is this relational dynamic of *agapē* that Christ sets forth as the foremost commandment;[124] it is the very basis of our redemption;[125] and sanctification;[126] and, as such, it is the fountainhead of all other affections found within every child of God, as Jonathan Edwards correctly states:

> "For love is not only one of the affections, but it is the first and chief of the affections, and the fountain of all the affections." (Matt 22:37-40) [127]

The Christian is not a reconstituted devotee of *erōs*-love, but is a new creation in Christ[128] whereby the old things have passed away and *new things have come;* and it is the Spirit's first fruit of love which permeates every aspect of the Christian's life. This therefore constitutes the central conflict between worldly and godly affections that continues to this day, just as it did in Paul's

---

[123] Philippians 2:3-5: 3. Do nothing from selfishness or empty conceit, but with humility of mind regard one another as more important than yourselves; 4. do not merely look out for your own personal interests, but also for the interests of others. 5. Have this attitude in yourselves which was also in Christ Jesus,

[124] Mark 12:28-31.

[125] Ephesians 2:4.

[126] 1 John 4:19.

[127] Jonathan Edwards, A treatise concerning religious affections: (Oak Harbor, WA: Logos Research Systems, Inc., 1996).

[128] 2 Corinthians 5:17: 17. Therefore if anyone is in Christ, he is a new creature; the old things passed away; behold, new things have come.

day. Those who appeal to Lewis' writings, arguing that *agapē* and *erōs* resolve into one kind of love at their root, reveal a dangerous misunderstanding since *the very core idea of relational union in agapē is antithetical to erōs*. Moreover, as noted earlier, such an *agapē*-union is central to the Triune love of the Godhead.[129]

> John 17:22-24: 22. "The glory which You have given Me I have given to them, that they may be one, just as We are one; 23. I in them and You in Me, that they may be perfected in unity, so that the world may know that You sent Me, and loved them, even as You have loved Me. 24. "Father, I desire that they also, whom You have given Me, be with Me where I am, so that they may see My glory which You have given Me, for You loved Me before the foundation of the world."

The beauty of Trinitarian love infinitely transcends human comprehension. However, what the child of God can and must understand is that, *as His children,* we enjoy the intimacy and union of love which the Father sets upon His own Son, whom He calls *the Beloved.*[130] As well, this love that He *freely* sets upon us, as a gift of His grace, establishes the very nature of our walk in this world. Consider Paul's important call to sanctification in Ephesians chapter 5. Much of this chapter speaks of the wickedness that the children of God are to avoid, but the ultimate foundation of his argument is rooted in our loving relationship with the Lord as His *beloved* children:

> Ephesians 5:1-2: 1. Therefore be imitators of God, as beloved children; 2. and walk in love, just as Christ also loved you and gave

---

[129] John 14:31, John 10:17
[130] Ephesians 1:6.

Himself up for us, an offering and a sacrifice to God as a fragrant aroma...8. for you were formerly darkness, but now you are Light in the Lord; walk as children of Light 9. (for the fruit of the Light consists in all goodness and righteousness and truth), 10. trying to learn what is pleasing to the Lord.

A child who loves his Father *truly* will *learn what is pleasing* to Him. For the children of God, this focus on God's pleasures unveils the reality of such a loving *relationship*. Without such a union in Christ, we are left to our worldliness and fleshly pleasures (Ephesians 5:3-7, 11-16). The impact of mixing *erōs* and *agapē* would devastate the meaning of what we have just examined:

- **Christ sacrificed Himself out of His infinite love for the Father (John 1:1, 8; 14:31; 17:24):** *Ephesians 5:2 "...Christ...gave Himself up...a sacrifice to God as a fragrant aroma..."*

- **Christ sacrificed Himself out of His love for His people:** *Ephesians 5:2 "...Christ also loved you and gave Himself up for us..."*

- **Christ sacrificed Himself for our spiritual adoption:** *Ephesians 5:1 "Therefore be imitators of God, as beloved children..."*

The relational emphasis of Christ's *agapē*-love runs throughout these verses. We are *beloved* children and therefore the Lord is ours, not by personal merit, but by the *free expression of His grace, mercy, and adopting love*. When Paul enjoins us to *"...walk in love, just as Christ also loved you..."* his call of imitation is made very clear. The Greek comparative particle, *kathōs*, establishes the standard of comparison: we are to walk in love *just as* Christ has walked as the greatest example of love in all of human history. His fulfillment of the foremost commandment was carried out in perfect obedience[131] through His eternal union of love with the Father, offering Himself as a fragrant aroma on our behalf *to God*. Without such a relational union of love, within the Trinity and towards us, we would have no hope of redemption whatsoever. The centrality of God's love must never be underestimated; nor should it ever be redacted in order to appeal to worldly appetites. In view of all this, consider once again the confusing doctrine of love advanced by Bell:

> *"God is that loving. If we want isolation, despair, and the right to be our own god, God graciously grants us that option."*[132]

Bell's contorted definitions are the byproducts of a subjectively defined notion of love. Similar to Lewis, Bell's definitions of love and freedom are *anthropocentric*, rather than *theocentric*. However, despite Bell's confident assertions, God's love is very different from the base affections of men. The true love of God is that which freely and effectually draws men *away from their lust, rather than giving them over to it.* When theologians endeavor to whitewash the reality of God's just wrath and judgment, they leave themselves with a damnable half-truth. Ultimately, an emphasis on self-oriented love fosters subjectivism, and leads the individual to believe that the centerpiece of worship, Heaven, and Hell revolves around man, not God. Clearly, Bell's presentation of God's love and grace is entirely antithetical to the notion of *agapē*-love.

---

[131] John 10:17.
[132] Rob Bell, Love Wins, p. 12.

It is crucial to understand that Christian love is not the world's *erōs*. It is grounded in a supernatural union with the One who died in our stead out of His great love for His Father,[133] and for His chosen bride.[134] Should the church fail to communicate these precious truths well, she may run the risk of reducing her message of hope to something far less - as in the case of Rob Bell and C.S. Lewis. Much more is at stake than we tend to comprehend. Within this world of self-esteem and self-satisfaction, we should admit that the world knows little else but the desire of *erōs*. In fact, this is the only "love" that they can know apart from *union with Christ*. Thus, *agapē*-love is not a warmed-over version of selfishness; instead, it is the central component to our new life in, and union with, the Savior who first loved us. This very love is the love *of God* that has been poured out in our hearts.[135] The men of this world worship at their altars to an unknown love and an unknown god, and as we shall see in the next chapter, the natural man's false conception of *love* and *freedom* stands in conflict with some of the core tenants of the Gospel message. Thus, when we speak to others about the true God of love, we must be careful not to cloud our discussion with worldly words, concepts, and ideas in our attempt to share the Gospel.

When we consider the great need of the lost, we must remember the gravity of our task.

---

[133] John 14:31.

[134] Ephesians 5:25.

[135] Romans 5:5 ...and hope does not disappoint, because the love of God has been poured out within our hearts through the Holy Spirit who was given to us.

CHAPTER 4
THE FREEDOM
OF LOVE

> *"...the damned are under no obligation to return to Hell.*
> *They can stay on in Heaven if they wish-if they are willing*
> *to forego their most precious sins."*[136]
> *- The Great Divorce, Macmillan Publishing*

In the introduction, I mentioned the controversy over Rob Bell's book, *Love Wins*, in order to expose the reader to the problematic influences of Lewis' writings.[137] Providentially, the controversy surrounding Bell has yielded the benefit of uncovering the often undetected undercurrents of Lewis' influence. Similar to Lewis' *The Great Divorce*, Bell operates from a view of mankind which centralizes the notion of *human free will*. In public interviews, as well as in his book, he has repeated the assertion that *God is love and love demands freedom*. It is essential that we decipher his statement, remembering that Bell's definition of love is defective at the root level. For Bell, the centerpiece of his love-equation is not God, but man. Thus, when he speaks of *love*, he refers to God's love *for mankind*; and when he speaks of freedom, he again speaks of the notion of *human free will*. In fact, I would even extend that thought to say that Bell seems to present this view of free will with the fervor that is normally associated with

---

[136] Macmillan Publishing Co., publisher's summary of The Great Divorce by C.S. Lewis, back cover.

[137] There are other examples of Lewis' systemic influence on the modern, professing church including the ecumenical work: *Evangelicals & Catholics Together*, by Charles Colson and Richard John Neuhaus. In chapter 1, *The Common Cultural Task*, Colson reveals his central devotion to Lewis when he says: "'Evangelicals and Catholics Together' seeks to continue the legacy of C.S. Lewis..." Charles Colson and Richard John Neuhaus eds., Evangelicals and Catholics Toghether, Towards a Common Mission (Dallas Texas: Word Publishing, 1995), p. 36.

CHAPTER 4 - THE FREEDOM OF LOVE

Open Theism.[138] In both cases, the idea of human freedom is so strongly guarded that everything else is mutilated in the process - *especially the nature of God*. A God who waits passively, submissively, and even ignorantly for all future, yet unknown, free-choices of men is no God at all. Yet, this reflects the system of thinking upheld in *The Great Divorce*, and it is the same form of thinking reproduced within *Love Wins*. What we know from church history, and from Bell's book, is that those who exalt a notion of human freedom end up mutilating the reality of God's ultimate freedom and sovereignty over everything. Thus, when theologians of this stripe speak of God's love, it is no longer a free, sovereign, and electing love which acts independently of man's will; but it is a kind of love that must act *dependently and subordinately* to the higher freedom of man. Bell's defense of such an immutable human freedom comes in a very interesting way. As noted earlier, Bell repeats the question - "Does God get what He wants?" over the span of several pages in *Love Wins*, but then chooses to drop this question, instantly, for what he calls a "better question":[139]

> "But there's a better question, one we can answer, one that takes all of this speculation about the future, which no one has been to and then returned with hard, empirical evidence, and brings it back to

---

[138] This observation is made not only in view of Bell's teaching, but also in view of his preferred associations in *Love Wins*. Of the two endorsers published within *Love Wins*, Greg Boyd (a popular advocate of Open Theism) is given greatest prominence: "Love Wins is a bold, prophetic, and poetic masterpiece. I don't know any writer who expresses the inexpressible love of God as powerfully and as beautifully as Rob Bell! Many will disagree with some of Rob's perspectives, but no one who seriously engages this book will put it down unchanged. A 'must read' book!" Greg Boyd's endorsement of Love Wins by Rob Bell, back cover - inside flap.

[139] Bell, Love Wins, p. 116.

one absolute we can depend on in the midst of all of this, which turns out to be another question. It's not 'Does God get what God wants?' but 'Do we get what we want?' And the answer to that is a resounding, affirming, sure, and positive yes. Yes, we get what we want. God is that loving. If we want isolation, despair, and the right to be our own god, God graciously grants us that option. If we insist on using our God-given power and strength to make the world in our own image, God allows us that freedom; we have the kind of license to that. If we want nothing to do with light, hope, love, grace, and peace, God respects that desire on our part, and we are given a life free from any of those realities. The more we want nothing to do with all God is, the more distance and space are created. If we want nothing to do with love, we are given a reality free from love."[140]

This text is a clear sample of the confusing and contradicting nature of his entire book. Consider his logic concerning the relationship between human freedom and God's love:

Yes, we get what we want. God is that loving. If we want isolation, despair, and the right to be our own god, God graciously grants us that option....If we want nothing to do with love, we are given a reality free from love."[141]

According to Bell, the lost are *unloved* in *God's love*. Only a very strained nuance of meaning could produce statements like these, especially when we consider the true nature of God's love as defined by Scripture. Equally twisted is his understanding of God's grace. Exactly how could anyone argue that God's act of giving men over to their depraved desires is an act of love or grace? Only in an upside-down world of thinking can such

---

[140] Ibid.
[141] Ibid.

reasoning be generated. In reality, such "grace" isn't grace at all, instead it is God's just judgment against the wickedness of men (Romans 1). Yet, for Bell, it is grace because of God's supposed high regard for mankind's "free will." Bell's own exaltation of human freedom is disturbing, but not new. For him, the "one absolute we can depend on" is not: "Does God get what He wants?" instead it is "Do we get what we want?" Even Tim Keller, whom Bell cites in his Further Reading list, in *Love Wins*, yields a similar notion of the centrality of human freedom in the same spirit of Lewis:

> Modern people inevitably think that hell works like this: God gives us time, but if we haven't made the right choices by the end of our lives, he casts our souls into hell for all eternity. As the poor souls fall though space, they cry out for mercy, but God says "Too late! You had your chance! Now you will suffer!" This caricature misunderstands the very nature of evil...No one ever asks to leave hell. That is why it is a travesty to picture God casting people into a pit who are crying "I'm sorry! Let me out!"[142]

This is, in part, a reproduction of what is central to Lewis' work, *The Great Divorce*, where men remain in Hell *contingent upon their ongoing self-choice*:

> *"All that are in Hell choose it. Without that self-choice there could be no Hell."*[143]

---

[142] Timothy J. Keller, <u>The Reason for God:</u> *Belief in an Age of Skepticism*. (New York: Dutton, 2008), pp.76, 78-79. Keller's devotion to Lewis is rife in *The Reason for God* in addition to other works of his. It is for this reason that some have called him the "C.S. Lewis for the 21st century."

[143] Lewis, <u>The Great Divorce</u>, p., 72.

It is this idea of a *self-created* and *self-sustained*[144] Hell that dominates Bell's book from the beginning. According to Bell, the ongoing free will of men, not the eternal judgment of God, is the basis for someone *remaining in Hell*. We also see this in his summary of the parable of the rich man and Lazarus (Luke 16:19-31):

> "...note what it is the [rich] man wants in hell: he wants Lazarus to get him water. When you get someone water, you're serving them. The rich man wants Lazarus to serve him. In their previous life, the rich man saw himself as better than Lazarus, and now, in hell, the rich man *still* sees himself as above Lazarus. It's no wonder Abraham says there's a chasm that can't be crossed. The chasm is the rich man's heart!...He's still clinging to the old hierarchy. He still thinks he's better."[145]

With this interpretation in place, Bell continues to press a view of Hell in which its inhabitants remain there *only because of their ongoing free will and choice.* The chasm that exists between Heaven and Hell is sustained by the will of man, rather than the eternal and final judgment of God.

---

[144] Lewis' emphasis on human freedom leads him to conclude that the inhabitants of Hell will *enjoy the freedom they have demanded*. Thus the permanence of their condemnation depends upon their own desire for freedom: "I willingly believe that the damned are, in one sense, successful, rebels to the end; that the doors of hell are locked on the inside. I do not mean that the ghosts may not wish to come out of hell, in the vague fashion wherein an envious man 'wishes' to be happy: but they certainly do not will even the first preliminary stages of that self-abandonment through which alone the soul can reach any good. They enjoy forever the horrible freedom they have demanded, and are therefore self-enslaved." C.S. Lewis, The Problem of Pain (HarperOne, New York, NY, 2001), p. 130.

[145] Bell, Love Wins, p. 77.

Thus, everything is a cycle of man's free will.

No mention is made by Bell about the fact that the rich man was so filled with torment and remorse over his condition that his ultimate desire was to have his remaining brothers warned about the very real place of torment in which he now resided. This would not have fit well within Bell's *story* about what he calls Heaven and Hell. Thus, when Bell speaks of this life and the life to come, his argument converges to this thought of subjective human experience as being that which defines Heaven and Hell, thus diminishing the thought of the objective reality of God's judgment. In what might be called - *Potential Universal Restoration*[146] - Bell raises the prospect of Hell having a purgatorial function[147] such that a "period of pruning...a time of trimming...or an intense experience of correction"[148] will take place for those, like the rich man, whose separation from God is sustained only by their continued preference for Hell. This form of thinking is further advanced in Chapter 7 where Bell presents his version of the Prodigal Son, in which he essentially argues - *Hell is what you make it to be - in this life and in the life to come.* This same notion of the centrality of man's will is reflected in Lewis' fictional bus ride from Hell to Heaven, in *The Great Divorce*, where those who want Hell can go back to it; but those

---

[146] Origin held to the view of Universal Restoration where the afterlife has a purgatorial function, such that, "...when there has been a sufficient period of punishment, mankind will be purified to the point where God may have fellowship with them throughout the remainder of eternity." Millard Erickson, Christian Theology, (Baker Book House), p. 1017.

[147] Bell, Love Wins, pp. 85-93.

[148] Ibid., p. 91.

who want to take the omnibus from Hell to Heaven can do so as well, as evidenced in this fictional exchange.

> *"...what of the poor Ghosts who never get into the omnibus at all?"*
>
> *"Everyone who wishes it does...No soul that seriously and constantly desires joy will ever miss it. Those who seek find. To those who knock it is opened."*[149]

Thinking such as this corresponds strongly to Bell's continued arguments throughout the book, especially in Chapter 5, *Dying to Live*, and Chapter 7 *The Good News is Better than That*.

I do believe that all of the attention given to Bell's teaching on Hell has served as a distraction from other important issues. Because of this we could say that his teachings on Hell have been a left jab to the right hook of what he does to the nature of God's love in *Love Wins*. Much of his book comes off as an angry rant against a God who would dare to send unregenerate men and women to an everlasting Hell, devoid of the possibility of purgatorial restoration. Thus, Bell perpetuates several historic and faulty notions regarding God's holiness, human depravity, and God's justice:

---

[149] Lewis, The Great Divorce., pp. 72-73. We should also note that Lewis elsewhere speaks of the inhabitants of Hell as having a shrinking humanity, such that they are no longer men at all: "We know much more about heaven than hell, for heaven is the home of humanity and therefore contains all that is implied in a glorified human life: but hell was not made for men. It is in no sense parallel to heaven: it is 'the darkness outside', the outer rim where being fades away into nonentity." Lewis, The Problem of Pain, p. 129.

CHAPTER 4 - THE FREEDOM OF LOVE

> "Millions have been taught that if they don't believe, if they don't accept in the right way, that is, the way the person telling them the gospel does, and they were hit by a car and died later that same day, God would have no choice but to punish them forever in conscious torment in hell. God would, in essence, become a fundamentally different being to them in that moment of death, a different being to them *forever*. A loving heavenly father who will go to extraordinary lengths to have a relationship with them would, in the blink of an eye, become a cruel, mean, vicious tormenter who would ensure that they had no escape from an endless future of agony. If there was an earthly father who was like that, we would call the authorities. If there was an actual human dad who was that volatile, we would contact child protection services immediately. If God can switch gears like that, switch entire modes of being that quickly, that raises a thousand questions about whether a being like this could ever be trusted, let alone be good."[150]

Sadly, Bell can barely contain his disgust over the conjoined reality of the *kindness and severity of God*:[151]

> "...if your God is loving one second and cruel the next, if your God will punish people for all of eternity for sins committed in a few short years, no amount of clever marketing or compelling language, or good music, or great coffee, will be able to disguise that one, true, glaring, untenable, unacceptable, awful reality."[152]

It is here that we see the transitive influence of Lewis' master, George MacDonald:

---

[150] Bell, Love Wins, pp. 173-74.
[151] Romans 11:22: Behold then the kindness and severity of God; to those who fell, severity, but to you, God's kindness, if you continue in His kindness; otherwise you also will be cut off.
[152] Ibid., p. 175.

"Punishment, I repeat, is not the thing required of God, but the absolute destruction of sin. What better is the world, what better is the sinner, what better is God, what better is the truth, that the sinner should suffer--continue suffering to all eternity? Would there be less sin in the universe? Would there be any making-up for sin? ...What setting-right would come of the sinner's suffering? If justice demand it, if suffering be the equivalent for sin, then the sinner must suffer, then God is bound to exact his suffering, and not pardon; and so the making of man was a tyrannical deed, a creative cruelty."[153]

A key component to MacDonald's reasoning is his conflation of the words: *justice and mercy.* Beginning with Psalm 62:12, MacDonald makes some key modifications:

Psalm 62:12 Also unto Thee, O Lord, belongeth mercy [*ḥesed*]; for Thou renderest to every man according to his work.

Despite the fact that the Hebrew word for mercy in this text is *ḥesed* (*mercy, lovingkindness*), MacDonald insists that it would be better to understand the text as: "Also unto thee, O Lord, belongeth *justice*..."[154] After this substitution, he then argues for a monolithic idea of justice as denoting reconciliation. With these components in his equation, he then concludes that God's dealing with the human race is grounded in an effort of achieving a salvific and universal reconciliation of men as an act of justice. As he works backwards from this idea, he then surmises that the idea of Hell and torment is utterly incomprehensible. Once again, the transitive influence of MacDonald upon Bell is evident through a disdain for the

---

[153] George MacDonald's sermon: Justice.

[154] "I believe that justice and mercy are simply one and the same thing..." Ibid.

concept of God's just wrath against sinners, *forever*. This form of thinking leads both men into fields of reasoning not at all dissimilar to that of humanism. In fact, when reading *Love Wins*, I was frequently reminded of the humanism of Christopher Hitchens as advanced in his book - *god is not Great*. Hitchens' complaints about the concepts of Heaven, Hell, and the judgment of God against sinners, were frequent and filled with obvious disdain. For Hitchens, such thinking was repulsive and led him, in part, to conclude - *I'll have nothing to do with such a "god."* It is for this reason that, while engrossed in my reading of *Love Wins*, I had to stop and remind myself which of the two books I had in my hands. When one distills the *humanism* of Hitchens' arguments, it becomes evident that each man is writing from the same twisted *art and thought of man* in their attempt to rid the Universe of a wrathful and just God.[155] The only difference is that Hitchens, to his credit, didn't try to use Scripture as a *truthful basis* for his faulty arguments. When addressing the subject of Hell itself, along with the question of its duration, Bell only consults his subjective sense of logic on the matter, arguing (as does Christopher Hitchens) that such a just and wrathful God *is not great*:

Hitchens: "[Re: God's judgment of men in the book of Revelation (14:20)] - "...it can always be egotistically hoped that one will be personally spared [of such final judgment], gathered contentedly to

---

[155] Acts 17:29: 29. "Being then the children of God, we ought not to think that the Divine Nature is like gold or silver or stone, an image formed by the art and thought of man.

the bosom of the mass exterminator, and from a safe place observe the sufferings of those less fortunate."[156]

Bell, as cited earlier: "... if your God will punish people for all of eternity for sins committed in a few short years, no amount of clever marketing or compelling language, or good music, or great coffee, will be able to disguise that one, true, glaring, untenable, unacceptable, awful reality."[157]

The overlap of thinking between Hitchens and Bell is striking. Both of these men regard the idea of God's just and holy wrath against unrepentant sinners as untenable. However, as Bell has already admitted, this is not new at all: the Apostle Paul invested much ink and papyri in order to remind his readers that there is no injustice within the God who exercises such wrath and justice:

Romans 3:5-6: 5...The God who inflicts wrath is not unrighteous, is He? (I am speaking in human terms.) 6. May it never be! For otherwise, how will God judge the world?

The Apostle also reminds us that those who argue against this truth do so as mere clay pots who boastfully answer back against the Potter;[158] and the fact that God actually has a *divine*

---

[156] Christopher Hitchens, god is not Great, (Twelve, New York, 2007), p. 56. Hitchens frequently skips around from one sampling to another in his book. In this particular citation, Hitchens quotes portions from the book of Revelation chapter 14, and then complains that it is "sheer manic relish, larded with half-quotations...One of the very many connections between religious belief and the sinister, spoiled, selfish childhood of our species is the repressed desire to see everything smashed up and ruined and brought to naught."

[157] Bell, Love Wins, p.175.

[158] Romans 9:20-22.

purpose in such judgment produces even more vitriol within their hearts.[159] Sadly, in the modern day, it has become fashionable, once again, to question God's authority in such judgment. Those who have argued thus do so with the faulty premise that such judgment is *purposeless*, revealing a kind of error and waste in the divine plan. We even see traces of this in the writings of men like N.T. Wright:

> *"...the covenant between God and Israel was always designed to be God's means of saving the whole world. It was never supposed to be the means whereby God would have a private little group of people who would be saved while the rest of the world went to hell (whatever you might mean by that). Thus, when God is faithful to the covenant in the death and resurrection of Jesus Christ and in the work of the Spirit, it makes nonsense of the Pauline gospel to imagine that the be-all and end-all of this operation is so that God can have another, merely different, private little group of people who are saved while the world is consigned to the cosmic waste-paper basket."*[160]

What N.T. Wright presents in this text bears a strong family likeness to Hitchens' and Bell's own point - that the historic doctrine of Hell is *untenable and unacceptable*. Similarly, for Bell and Wright, the logic of their arguments boils down to this idea: without the possibility of a final reconciliation of mankind, the concept of Hell is unworthy of any serious consideration. Thus, we might say that *humanism "wins"* with such a doctrinal innovation. What is ultimately lost in all of these forms of reasoning is the reality of God's ultimate freedom in everything: the freedom of His justice, the freedom of His mercy, and the

---

[159] Romans 9:23-24.
[160] N.T. Wright, What Saint Paul Really Said, (William B. Eerdmans Publishing Company, Gran Rapids, MI, 1997), p. 163.

freedom of His *agapē*-love. We might agree with Bell that *God is love and love demands freedom*, if by freedom we mean the ultimate freedom of the sovereign Lord of all. However, there is no solution to be had in a system of thought that exalts human freedom above the Lord Himself. The free expression of God's love leads men, not into the abyss of their *erōs*-love and selfishness, but instead into an eternal union of adoption as His children, and as the bride of Christ. As the subjects of His glorious kingdom, we will never again become slaves to lust and the corruption of the flesh.

Such is true freedom.

The sad reality is that the writings of these men, as consumed by many, offer a false form of hope. Bell's opportunity to teach a wide audience about the love of God in his book, *Love Wins*, resulted in a gross debacle before a world audience. Had Mr. Bell *reasoned from the scriptures* in his treatment of the subjects of God's love, Heaven, Hell, and the eternal state, then he would have had a precious opportunity to magnify Christ through the Gospel. Nevertheless, his artistic and Lewis-like philosophical reasoning, his experiential musings, and his subjective thinking obfuscated everything. It is quite sad to see someone descending into the depths of his own thinking to such an extent that his message bears no significant difference to that of an Atheist.

When a man's message is so deeply gutted as this, he becomes an inferior messenger, not just among the living, but even among the damned - as we will see next in our conclusion - *A Solemn Message from Hell.*

CONCLUSION

A SOLEMN MESSAGE

FROM HELL

> *"...I beg you, father, that you send him to my father's house—for I have five brothers—in order that he may warn them, so that they will not also come to this place of torment.'*
> *- Luke 16:27-28*

We come to our conclusion with the following from Mr. Bell himself:

> "...we create hell whenever we fail to trust God's retelling of our story. The older brother's failure to trust, we learn, is rooted in his distorted view of God. There is a problem with his 'God.'"[161]

What I find partially agreeable in his statement is this: there is a great danger whenever we create our own "god" in the image of our own "responses and discussions and debates and opinions and longings and desires and wisdom and insights."[162] Agreeing with this one point of his, I would remind Mr. Bell of the violence that he has done to the very nature of God in his constant effort to preserve and protect his notion of human freedom. His mantra of: *"God is love, and love demands freedom,"* may be appealing to the masses, but it is not the Gospel. I offer this as an exhortation and warning for us all. Our need is not found in the white spaces of Scripture; what we need is God's eternal and immutable truth, as the psalmist said:

Psalm 119:92: If Your law had not been my delight, then I would have perished in my affliction.

---

[161] Bell, Love Wins, p. 173.
[162] Ibid., p. X (Preface).

Without absolute truth, we do perish. The dangerous game played by those who revel in *extrabiblical reasoning* and *inductive uncertainty* is one that endangers the souls of men. Thus, this is no game at all. The biblical teachings about Heaven and Hell are pivotal matters, and must never be obfuscated in the presence of this world. In addition, as already argued, the doctrine of God's free and sovereign love is intensely precious, being central to the message of the Gospel itself. Men have no hope within themselves, nor in an imagined place of purgatorial reconciliation. Without the Love of God manifested in the person of Jesus Christ, who was sacrificed on the cross as a substitute for many; bearing their sins and the penalty due for their sins; standing in their stead as a righteous advocate and covering every believer with the perfection of His sinless obedience - without *Him*, we have *no hope*. The gravity of the message of God's love and mercy in the person and work of Christ is nothing with which one should trifle; therefore, within our entertainment-crazed culture we must never forget the seriousness of such a message.

Everything centers on the message of Christ.

The Christian must not try to appease this culture's addiction to entertainment and humor, nor is it to overcompensate with a dry and spiritless proclamation. We see these extremes quite often in the present day, the most popular of which is the Christian-as-court-jester motif. However, if there is a central attitude in the Apostolic preaching of the Gospel, it is this: *solemnity*. I state this, not as a matter of guesswork or personal opinion; instead, I state this as a clear principle of Scripture.

The frequency and centrality of this concept of solemnity is compelling (italics mine):

- **Peter's solemn preaching of the Gospel in Jerusalem:** Acts 2:40: And with many other words he *solemnly testified* and kept on exhorting them, saying, "Be saved from this perverse generation!"

- **Peter's description of his commission to preach:** Acts 10:42: And He ordered us to preach to the people, and *solemnly to testify* that this is the One who has been appointed by God as Judge of the living and the dead.

- **Paul's ministry to the Corinthians:** Acts 18:5: But when Silas and Timothy came down from Macedonia, Paul began devoting himself completely to the word, *solemnly testifying* to the Jews that Jesus was the Christ.

- **Paul's faithful ministry amidst the Ephesians:** Acts 20:21-24: - 21. *solemnly testifying* to both Jews and Greeks of repentance toward God and faith in our Lord Jesus Christ. 22. "And now, behold, bound by the Spirit, I am on my way to Jerusalem, not knowing what will happen to me there, 23. except that the Holy Spirit *solemnly testifies* to me in every city, saying that bonds and afflictions await me. 24. "But I do not consider my life of any account as dear to myself, so that I may finish my course and the ministry which I received from the Lord Jesus, *to testify solemnly* of the gospel of the grace of God.

- **Christ's exhortation to Paul:** Acts 23:11: But on the night immediately following, the Lord stood at his side and said,

"Take courage; for as you have *solemnly witnessed* to My cause at Jerusalem, so you must witness at Rome also."

- **Paul's continued ministry in Rome:** Acts 28:23: When they had set a day for Paul, they came to him at his lodging in large numbers; and he was explaining to them by *solemnly testifying* about the kingdom of God and trying to persuade them concerning Jesus, from both the Law of Moses and from the Prophets, from morning until evening.

Say what you will about the proper techniques for sharing the Gospel. If there is one clear pattern found within the attitudes of the Apostles it is this: *solemnity*.

Solemnity does not mean being morose and gloomy, and it certainly does not mean acting like a clown. What it means is that we as Christians ought to proclaim the joyful message of the Good News with all the gravity and sobriety that it deserves, for there is no greater "news" in all of creation. Moreover, I should note that the conjoining of *joy* and *solemnity* renders no contradiction,[163] though some may claim that it does. As the citizens of God's eternal kingdom, we have the true joy of Christ being made full in ourselves,[164] and this, *by contrast*, gives us a profound knowledge of this world's dark and perilous state. This despairing condition of humanity ought to bring great sobriety to the heart of every true saint. Ultimately, a drowning victim requires a serious rescuer and a sure rope, not an unequipped jokester. The good news that we proclaim is that

---

[163] Psalm 2:11 Worship the Lord with reverence and rejoice with trembling.

[164] John 17:13: "But now I come to You; and these things I speak in the world so that they may have My joy made full in themselves."

the Gospel's length and strength has sufficient power to pull others out of their otherwise certain destruction.

Yes, the Gospel is serious.

What I present here is nothing new, and is even presented with great force in Bunyan's classic, Pilgrim's Progress:

> Christian saw the picture of a very grave person hang up against the wall; and this was the fashion of it: It had eyes lifted up to heaven, the best of books in his hand, the law of truth was written upon its lips, the world was behind its back; it stood as if it pleaded with men, and a crown of gold did hang over its head.[165]

Bunyan's portrait of the godly preacher begins and ends with a description of his *solemnity*: he was *a very grave person* who *pleaded* with men. I would submit that this very portrait, which is wonderfully scriptural, is becoming the antithesis of the jesting, entertaining, cursing, and titillating preacher of the modern day. The message delivered by such preachers is one which belies the true gravity of the Gospel.

This leads us to a final, sad, and disturbing point of irony.

The aforementioned list of references, containing the word *diamarturōmai* (*solemnly testify*), is not at all exhaustive. In fact, there is another verse that contains this word and it comes from a rather unexpected source. It is supplied, not by an

---

[165] Bunyan, J. (1995). The Pilgrim's Progress : From this world to that which is to come. Oak Harbor, WA: Logos Research Systems, Inc.

Apostle, prophet, or evangelist; instead, it comes from the very pit of Hell:

> Luke 16:19-28: - 19. "Now there was a rich man, and he habitually dressed in purple and fine linen, joyously living in splendor every day. 20. "And a poor man named Lazarus was laid at his gate, covered with sores, 21. and longing to be fed with the crumbs which were falling from the rich man's table; besides, even the dogs were coming and licking his sores. 22. "Now the poor man died and was carried away by the angels to Abraham's bosom; and the rich man also died and was buried. 23. "In Hades he lifted up his eyes, being in torment, and saw Abraham far away and Lazarus in his bosom. 24. "And he cried out and said, 'Father Abraham, have mercy on me, and send Lazarus so that he may dip the tip of his finger in water and cool off my tongue, for I am in agony in this flame.' 25. "But Abraham said, 'Child, remember that during your life you received your good things, and likewise Lazarus bad things; but now he is being comforted here, and you are in agony. 26. 'And besides all this, between us and you there is a great chasm fixed, so that those who wish to come over from here to you will not be able, and that none may cross over from there to us.' 27. "And he said, 'Then I beg you, father, that you send him to my father's house— 28. for I have five brothers—in order that *he may warn* them [*diamarturētai*], so that they will not also come to this place of torment.' (italics mine).

I find it disturbingly ironic, and deeply challenging, when considering the solemnity of the inhabitants of Hell. Who else could comprehend the seriousness of the Gospel call and warning than those who face the actual consequences of rejecting Christ? To be frank, the parable of the Rich man and Lazarus is quite compelling, and flies in the face of the pop theologies of C.S. Lewis, George MacDonald, Rob Bell, and others like Brian McLaren, and Tony Campolo:

"I come out of a tradition that pays attention to George MacDonald and C.S. Lewis, and I'm contending that we need to deal with this question: Is God less just than I am, or is his sense of justice different than mine? It's very simple, MacDonald and Lewis would say, "There is a hell, there has to be, because if there is no hell, there is no freedom." In Lewis's book, The Great Divorce, he says, *'The bus leaves heaven every half hour, and anybody who doesn't want to stay in heaven goes to hell . . .* by his own choice!'"[166]

The Lewis/MacDonald view of Hell is not at all new, but continues to be popularized, whether intentionally or unintentionally, through the endorsements of prominent men. It may be popular to argue that some men will want to be in Hell, but it would appear that the actual inhabitants of Hell would beg to differ. In fact, if they could, they would have others go and preach the Gospel with *great solemnity.*

Finally, in Rob Bell's promotional video for *Love Wins*, he raised a question concerning whether or not Gandhi is in Hell. A question such as this is inherently problematic since knowledge of the eternal destiny of any individual soul is the prerogative of God alone. Yet, we are encouraged by the truth concerning that thief on the cross who trusted Christ in the final moments of his life. Just before his life in this world ended, he was redeemed and given the promise of life with Christ:

Luke 23:39-43: 39. One of the criminals who were hanged there was hurling abuse at Him, saying, "Are You not the Christ? Save Yourself

---

[166] Out of Ur, Brian McLaren's Inferno: the provocative church leader explains his view of hell (May 5th, 2006):
http://www.outofur.com/archives/2006/05/brian_mclarens.html, italics mine.

and us!" 40. But the other answered, and rebuking him said, "Do you not even fear God, since you are under the same sentence of condemnation? 41. "And we indeed are suffering justly, for we are receiving what we deserve for our deeds; but this man has done nothing wrong." 42. And he was saying, "Jesus, remember me when You come in Your kingdom!" 43. And He said to him, "Truly I say to you, today you shall be with Me in Paradise."

Christ was crucified along with two criminals: one who repented and believed in Him, and another who did not. In a sense, the whole reality of *Heaven, Hell, and the fate of every person who ever lived* is illustrated through both of these men. The criminal who did believe demonstrated four core convictions:

1. He feared God as the just Judge of all ("Do you not even fear God...?)

2. He knew that he was a miserable sinner and deserved judgment, thus he *solemnly warned* the other thief of this truth ("...we indeed are suffering justly, for we are receiving what we deserve for our deeds...").

3. He believed in Christ's purity and innocence ("...this man [Jesus] has done nothing wrong.")

4. He trusted Christ as the Redeemer, who alone could save his lost soul (Jesus, remember me when You come in Your kingdom!).

Just moments before his physical demise, this criminal who placed his faith in Christ experienced a miracle. His wretched and filthy sins were placed on the innocent Savior who hung there next to him. In that moment, the believing thief was pardoned of all of his transgressions, committed throughout all of his life, and was given the sure promise of eternal life with Christ on the sole basis of Jesus' perfect innocence and righteousness. Moreover, Christ suffered much more than the torment of the nails, the cross, and His crown of thorns: He bore the just wrath of the Father for the sins of all who are His through faith - including the believing thief who hung there beside Him. Solely on the basis of that substitutionary sacrifice of Christ, the believing thief was delivered from the surety of an eternal torment in Hell and he was given the promise of Paradise *just moments before breathing his last breath in this world.*

So what does this have to do with Gandhi?

A great deal. The lesson of the believing thief is very important. It reminds us that the grace of God's salvation is so great and powerful that any sinner can be forgiven of any sin at any time through faith in Jesus Christ. Because of this, there should be no doubt that there will be men and women in Heaven who resisted Christ throughout their lives, yet, before their final passing, repented of their sins and believed in the Savior. In some cases, this reality will be hidden from public knowledge, but will be revealed in the final judgment and redemption of mankind. There are many things that we must consign to mystery when we speak of the eternal destinies of those who have passed from this life. Otherwise, questions such as these often lead to vain speculations and distractions from more important issues. As for Gandhi, we can say with certainty that if he repented of his sin and believed in Christ before his death, then he too is in Paradise with Christ, along with the believing thief, *Lazarus*, and all those who have trusted in God's promised Redeemer. But if he did not, then he now abides with the unbelieving thief, *the rich man*, and all those who have perished apart from Christ. If this is the case, then Gandhi, along with all the other inhabitants of Hell, would have those of us who remain in this life warn the lost about the horrific torments of Hell. But until God's judgment comes, the question about Gandhi simply cannot be answered.

When we share Christ with others, it is crucial that we remember the precious example of the Apostles who *solemnly testified* on behalf of Christ. However, we should also recall the tormented souls of the damned. They are probably more disgusted with the machinations of liberal theology than we ever could be; and therefore, their understanding of the solemnity of the Gospel is something from which we ourselves could learn. As the Apostle Paul said:

> 2 Corinthians 5:11 Therefore, knowing the fear of the Lord, we persuade men...

In conclusion, our message to the world is a message of grave warning, genuine hope, and unspeakable Gospel joy. It is a message of the One true Creator who, out of His infinite mercy, grace, and *eternal love*, calls sinners to come to Him and enter into a loving *union* with Him forever without end, through faith in Jesus Christ the Lord. Such a love as this does not abandon the sinner to an *erōs*-selfishness, but instead draws the sinner away from such corruption into a blissful relationship with the Triune God and Creator of all. Moreover, in eternal glory the inhabitants of Heaven will serve the Lord in *true freedom* as His *bond-servants*, where there will no longer be any curse, death, crying, or pain.[167] The Gospel is a message that has real power as the supernatural revelation of God, and has been sufficiently revealed to us in the pages of Holy Writ - not through the vain imaginations of mere men. For the Apostle Peter, this clarification was no small matter.

> 2 Peter 1:16: For we did not follow cleverly devised tales when we made known to you the power and coming of our Lord Jesus Christ, but we were eyewitnesses of His majesty.

The Gospel is no work of fiction; nor is it a fantasy; and it is not the product of the art and thought of man. Dear reader - these things I have shared with you "so that your faith would not rest on the wisdom of men, but on the power of God."[168]

---

[167] Revelation 22:3: There will no longer be any curse; and the throne of God and of the Lamb will be in it, and His bond-servants will serve Him; Revelation 21:4: ...and He will wipe away every tear from their eyes; and there will no longer be any death; there will no longer be any mourning, or crying, or pain; the first things have passed away."

[168] 1 Corinthians 2:4-5: 4. and my message and my preaching were not in persuasive words of wisdom, but in demonstration of the Spirit and of power, 5. so that your faith would not rest on the wisdom of men, but on the power of God.

APPENDIX

LOVE WINS - A MESSAGE OF UNCERTAINTY

"Is judgment not final? Is there really a way out of Hell into Heaven?"[169]

- C.S. Lewis to George MacDonald in The Great Divorce

Sadly, books of doctrinal depth and serious research have taken a backseat to the fluff and stuff of whatever is deemed as cool in this shallow age, and the moneychangers of the modern day have no apparent shame in transforming the *house of God* into a *publishing-house* of useless merchandise. What Bell has sold to the public is a kind of *impressionistic theology* – vague, ethereal, and utterly devoid of any objective reality. Sadly, such a work as this appeals to the masses who don't want to have to think very hard about the harsh realities of life and eternity, as if to conclude: *we need not worry about the choices made in this life, we will have an eternity to right our every wrong.* The writing choices of Bell, and the publishing choices of HarperOne, are at best disturbing and reveal the shallowness of the modern world of religious literature. In view of this, a few more things should be said about the messenger of *Love Wins,* and his message:

1. Rob Bell is more of an artist and story teller than a theologian. For him, story telling "has a powerful way of rescuing us from abstract theological discussions that can tie us up in knots for years."[170] As far as art is concerned, several pages are arranged with short, choppy statements which offer a graphic flare; and after a peculiar retelling of Christ's encounter with the rich young ruler (Luke 18), Bell

---

[169] Lewis: "Is judgment not final? Is there really a way out of Hell into Heaven?" MacDonald: "It depends on the way ye're using the words. If they leave that grey town behind it will not have been Hell. To any that leaves it, it is Purgatory." Lewis, The Great Divorce, p. 67.

[170] Bell, Love Wins, p. 12.

concludes with: "Try and paint *that*."[171] For this reason, I must say that the attempt to read and critique a book like this would not be terribly dissimilar to someone trying to interpret an abstract painting. With very little meaning and clarity within the presentation, the interpreter is left with a difficult task, and the creator of such "art" is left with enough play room to adjust his interpretation as needed, which leads me to a second point:

2. Bell's book is painted with broad brushes upon a canvas made of multiple questions, few of which he ever attempts to answer. There are even some questions that are strongly elevated for a while, but then quickly discarded for the sake of his overall presentation. Such an approach to theology is deeply characteristic of the Emergent Church community. Questions seem to be more important than answers, and Bell is bold enough to admit the need for creative license in the telling of the biblical "story," *as cited earlier*: "The ancient sages said the words of the sacred text were black letters on a white page - there's all that white space, waiting to be filled with our responses and discussions and debates and opinions and longings and desires and wisdom and insights. We read the words, and then enter into the discussion that has been going on for thousands of years across cultures and continents."[172] Bell hides precious little in this statement, and essentially admits to the reader at the very outset that his portrait of Heaven and Hell is not so much based upon Scripture as much as it is distilled from his "longings and desires and wisdom and insights." For this reason, I would strongly recommend that others avoid purchasing *Love Wins* entirely.

3. As already stated, Bell is not presenting anything that is dramatically new in his book. His own admission to this is fairly clear: "...please understand that nothing in this book hasn't been taught, suggested, or celebrated by many before me. I haven't come

---

[171] Ibid., 62.

[172] Ibid., p. X (Preface).

up with a radical new teaching that's any kind of departure from what's been said an untold number of times. That's the beauty of the historic, orthodox Christian faith. It's a deep, wide, diverse stream that's been flowing for thousands of years, carrying a staggering variety of voices, perspectives, and experiences."[173] As previously noted, the theological streams from which Bell draws are indeed old, but they are deeply troubling.

4. Bell's logic, and exegetical handling of the Scriptures is difficult to follow at times, but this is the product of his aforementioned affinity for *extrabiblical reasoning* and *inductive uncertainty*. This was already evident in his aforementioned use of the "white spaces" of the Word, which he said is "waiting to be filled with our responses and discussions and debates and opinions longings and desires and wisdom and insights." The most difficult aspect of this comes through Bell's loose treatment of the Scriptures themselves. Disciplined exegesis is not to be found within the pages of his book. As well, there are churlish moments such as this: "In Paul's first letter to Timothy he mentions Hymenaeus and Alexander, whom he has 'handed over to Satan to be taught not to blaspheme.' (Something in me wants to read that in a Darth Vader voice.)" To most of Bell's readers, this kind of writing may prove to be amusing, but comes off with a lightheartedness which belies a very serious concept: *handing rebellious men over to Satan for their discipline.*

5. Forthrightly, *Love Wins* is a fairly *undisciplined* work. This is not said as a matter of cruelty, but as a plain observation of what he has produced. *Love Wins* is a hodge-podge of disconnected scriptural references and thoughts, along with countless questions, emotive arguments, and scattered story telling. All this makes me wonder how such shoddy work can draw the respect and support of a large publishing house. It would appear that Bell's popularity, rather than his veracity and academic discipline, is the reason why he

---

[173] Ibid., p. X-XI (Preface)

commanded the attention of HarperOne. I am truly and honestly amazed that a manuscript such as this made it past an entry-level review.

As already noted, Bell maximizes uncertainty, and minimizes certainty, while maintaining a view of himself that he lies within the "wide, diverse stream" of Orthodox Christianity. The popularity of Bell's book, *Love Wins*, is both shocking and sad, and the thirty shekels of silver which HarperOne continues to collect from *Love Wins*, is bad money indeed. It would have been better if such a publishing choice had never been born.

But our examination of *Love Wins* has focused primarily on Bell's treatment of the subject of human freedom and the nature of God's love. The results of his thinking are most evident in the fact that men not only have unlimited freedom in this life, but even in the afterlife the inhabitants of Hell will be given purgatorial experiences that will, potentially, result in their transformation and transference from their own hellish experience - *if they choose to embrace such change.* However, the fact that he exalts the question - *do we get what we want?* - over his earlier query - *will God get what He wants?* – seems to suggest that his version of Universalism is one that is *potential* rather than *absolute*. This raises an important consideration about the subject of Universalism itself. There are variant strains of Universalism, and Bell seems to harvest his thinking from more than just one. In my observation, Bell draws out several components from the following historic categories of Universalism:

1. Universal Opportunity:[174] The distinction of this form of Universalism is focused on whether men and women can be saved apart from the special revelation of God. It is here that we see an added layer of Bell's views coming into play, such that the explicit message of the Gospel is redefined for a broader notion of *inclusivism*. "What Jesus does is declare that he, and he alone, is saving everybody. And then he leaves the door way, way open. Creating all sorts of possibilities. He is as narrow as himself and as wide as the universe. He is as exclusive as himself and as inclusive as containing every single particle of creation."[175] I should note here that Universal Opportunity does not necessarily mean that all will be saved in the end, but that all merely have the opportunity to be saved. This certainly is Bell's view, just as it was Lewis', as previously cited: *"There are people in other religions who are being led by God's secret influence to concentrate on those parts of their religion which are in agreement with Christianity, and who thus belong to Christ without knowing it. For example, a Buddhist of good will may be led to concentrate more and more on the Buddhist teaching about mercy and to leave in the background (though he might still say he believed) the Buddhist teaching on certain other points."*[176]

2. Universal Reconciliation: This view takes the thought of Universal atonement to its next logical step and sees the work of Christ as being *universally efficacious*. Therefore, "...the death of Christ made it possible for God to accept man, and he has done so. Consequently, whatever separation exists between man and the benefits of God's grace is subjective in nature; it exists only in man's mind."[177] Additionally, men must accept *practically* the

---

[174] Several of the categories used here are derived from Millard J. Erickson, Christian Theology, (Grand Rapids, Michigan: Baker Book House, 1992) pp. 1015-22.

[175] Bell, Love Wins, p. 157.

[176] Lewis, Mere Christianity, p., 209.

[177] Erickson, Christian Theology, p. 1017.

reconciliation that is theirs *positionally*. This form of thinking is, in part, contained within the argument which Bell posits; however, Bell does not go so far as to say that there will be a *practical reconciliation* for all men without exception: "Can God bring proper, lasting justice, banishing certain actions-and the people who do them-from the new creation while at the same time allowing and waiting and hoping for the possibility of the reconciliation of those very same people? Keeping the gates, in essence open? Will everyone eventually be reconciled to God or will there be those who cling to their version of their story, insisting on their right to be their own little god ruling their own little miserable kingdom? Will everybody be saved, or will some perish apart from God forever because of their choices? Those are questions, or more accurately, those are tensions we are free to leave fully intact. We don't need to resolve them or answer them because we can't, and so we simply respect them, creating space for the freedom that love requires."[178] By refusing to resolve the end result of God's supposed universal reconciliation of mankind, he shelters himself from the charge of holding to the traditional view of Universal Reconciliation - *just as Lewis does*. Bell's *partial* use of Universal Reconciliation is most evident in the 7th chapter of his book - *The Good News is Better than That*, where his retelling of the parable of the prodigal son is embedded in the idea that the father's love and forgiveness is already established, but the sons needed to discover and embrace that which was already theirs. His application of this is then applied to the whole of humanity. The Lord has already forgiven all,[179] but all do not yet understand and believe this. Their failure to believe and embrace this makes their lives *hellish*.[180] I would defer to Erickson at this point: "The message man needs to be told, then, is not that he has an

---

[178] Bell, Love Wins, p. 115.

[179] "Jesus forgives them all, without their asking for it." Ibid., p. 188.

[180] "...Jesus puts the older brother right there at the party, but refusing to trust the father's version of his story. Refusing to join in the celebration. Hell is being at the party. That's what makes it so hellish." Ibid., p. 169.

opportunity for salvation. Rather, man needs to be told that he has been saved, so that he may enjoy the blessings that are already his."[181] Concerning Bell, his conflicted reasoning results in the idea that there will be, potentially, saved and forgiven people who will remain in a state of *hellish* abandonment: "This makes what Jesus does in his story about the man with the two sons particularly compelling. Jesus puts the older brother right there at the party, but refusing to trust the father's version of his story. Refusing to join in the celebration. Hell is being at the party. That's what makes it so hellish."[182] By leaving the future open, as he does, he grants himself the license to slip away from the question of the eternal state of those who are "in Hell" - that is, Hell by Bell's definition. In some sense, Bell's arguments reveal a kind of worst case scenario of what can happen when universal atonement/reconciliation and human free will arguments are given complete reign. However, reconciliation, when used in a salvific sense, is clearly the propriety of God's chosen[183] and redeemed[184] people, as a gift of His grace. Had Bell presented more in the way of exegesis, he would have been delivered from his own logic:

3. Universal Restoration:[185] This is the view of Origen and its emphasis lies in the thought of *purgatorial restoration*. For Origen, the primacy of human free will made God's punishment of men in the afterlife pedagogic, rather than coercive. The end result would be

---

[181] Erickson, Christian Theology, p. 1017.

[182] Bell, Love Wins, p. 169.

[183] Colossians 1:1-2.

[184] Colossians 1:3-6.

[185] Origen employed the term: *apokatastasis* "restoration." - "Most notably connected with Origen of Alexandria (185–254), this Greek word refers to the teaching that all creation—even the devil himself—ultimately will be reconciled to God." Shedd, W. G. T., & Gomes, A. W. (2003). Dogmatic theology. "First one-volume edition (3 vols. in 1)"--Jacket. (3rd ed.) (952). Phillipsburg, N.J.: P & R Pub.

that all would, of their own volition and free will, turn to God.[186] For Origen, the idea of God's Universe being restored to its original condition is central, and Bell seems to reason for the potential of this in chapter five, *Dying to Live*. Bell begins with the story of his attendance at an Eminem concert, where he observed that the singer wore a cross around his neck. He then wonders, through his normal injection of questions, if the singer had gone through some metamorphosis, especially since he had practically disappeared as an artist for nearly five years. As Bell wanders through a maze of thoughts about the cycles of life and death, failure and renewal, he concludes with more questions about the possibility of the final restoration of the cosmos. This chapter is even more ethereal than the others, which is no small task, but in the end it fits within the broader canvas of his portrait of a kind of *potential Universal Restoration*. Bell's modification of Origen's view, as mentioned before, is made evident when he stops short of saying that all, without exception, will turn in the end.[187] Concerning this notion of purgatorial restoration, Bell conflates God's purposes in this life with the afterlife, indicating that Hell is a kind of perpetual second chance. In chapter 3 - *Hell*, he presents several examples of God's use of affliction, and even Satan himself, to chasten and turn the impenitent. No one could disagree with such a principle regarding God's work among men *in this life*; but what requires a great leap of faith is this notion that, in the afterlife, God will continue His program of correction, chastening, and ultimately, reconciliation. It is for this reason that Bell begins with a strained notion of the Greek word *aiōn*, arguing that Hell, both now, and in the afterlife, is to be

---

[186] "Most notably connected with Origen of Alexandria (185–254), this Greek word refers to the teaching that all creation—even the devil himself—ultimately will be reconciled to God." Ibid.

[187] "Will everybody be saved, or will some perish apart from God forever because of their choices? Those are questions...we are free to leave fully intact. We don't need to resolve them or answer them because we can't, and so we simply respect them, creating space for the freedom that love requires." Bell, Love Wins, p. 115.

seen as *purposeful states* within God's overall program of purgatorial restoration. But will God get what He wants? Well, remember, that's not a question that we can answer.[188]

Strictly speaking, Universalism *proper* requires the certainty that all will be drawn into Heaven at some point. Because Bell falls short of making a conclusive statement about the future, leaving such "tensions," as he says, "open" and unanswered, he leaves himself a bit of a back door from which he believes that he can reemerge as one who fits in with historic Christian orthodoxy:

> ***Shane Hipps of Mars Hill Bible Church:*** *"...I promise you when you get to read the book, you will find that it is fresh and liberating — but that it rests firmly in the wide screen of Orthodox Christianity and in the history of Christianity it fits perfectly. You will be very much at ease..."*[189]

This is pretty thin cover, and raises the question about Bell's understanding of the nature of God's knowledge and the effectual nature of His will: "...If we want hell, if we want heaven, they are ours. That's how love works. It can't be forced, manipulated, or coerced. It always leaves room for the other to

---

[188] But there's a better question...It's not 'Does God get what God wants?' but 'Do we get what we want?'...If we want isolation, despair, and the right to be our own god, God graciously grants us that option...The more we want nothing to do with all God is, the more distance and space are created. If we want nothing to do with love, we are given a reality free from love." Ibid., p. 116-17

[189] Eric Marrapodi, Firestorm grows over 'Christian heresy' book, (CNN Belief Blog):http://religion.blogs.cnn.com/2011/03/08/firestorm-over-bell-book-continues/?hpt=C2. Citation of Shane Hipps, Mars Hill Bible Church's teaching pastor, addressing the congregation about the theology of Bell's book, *Love Wins*.

decide. God says yes, we can have what we want, because love wins."[190] Bell frequently seeks refuge within the obscurity of an unknown future amidst his questions about the *openness* of our universe:

> "Are we the ultimate orbiter *[sic]* of what can, and cannot, exist? Or is the universe open, wondrous, unexpected, and far beyond anything we can comprehend? Are you open or closed?"[191]

Questioning such as this is typical for Bell, and is deeply embedded in his broader query about the future, and what God *might do* as a response to what we *might do*. Because of this, the reader is rarely left with convergent thoughts about eternity. If Bell believes that he has found a haven within Open Theism, one that preserves him from the charge of Universalism, then I would suggest that neither theological "shelter" will do him any good.

All of this is dangerous. Instead of warning men and women of the future and final judgment of God, we are left with a rather obscure and meaningless message. Instead of warning souls of the coming wrath of God, we are now offering a genteel discouragement from having a bummer experience at the party of Heaven - *whatever that means.* It is here that Bell's view on penal substitution is evident enough, or as he says: "Let's be very clear, then: we do not need to be rescued from God. God is the one who rescues us from death, sin, and destruction. God is the rescuer."[192]

---

[190] Bell, Love Wins, p. 61.
[191] Ibid.
[192] Ibid., p. 182.

LOVE WINS - A MISSED OPPORTUNITY
"Hell is a state of mind - ye never said a truer word."
- George MacDonald to C.S. Lewis,
in The Great Divorce[193]

With the recent crisis in Japan, and the world-unrest that prevails, it is crucial that Christians think very carefully about how to share the true message of hope with this despairing world. Rob Bell was given such an opportunity *via* national television on March 15th, 2011, with MSNBC's Martin Bashir and squandered the moment. To introduce the interview, Bashir began with the following:

> *"Before we come to talk about the book, let's talk about Japan. Which of these is true, either: God is all-powerful, but He doesn't care about the people of Japan and therefore their suffering, or...He does care about the people of Japan but He's not all-powerful...which one is it?"*

Though Bashir's question presents a false dilemma, it still was an excellent opportunity to present, on national TV, the biblical option that Bashir omitted. Instead, Bell responded with the all-too-predictable vagaries that we have come to expect from men like him. Rather than answering the question, he meandered within the reasoning found within his book, leaving Bashir with a non-response. Thus, Bashir persisted, but this time he failed

---

[193] This fictional quote of MacDonald comes after a broader dialogue between the two men. When they are introduced, Lewis reasserts his devotion to MacDonald's writings: "'My name is George,' he answered, 'George MacDonald.' 'Oh!' I cried. 'Then you can tell me! You at least will not deceive me.' Then, supposing that these expressions of confidence needed some explanation, I tried, trembling, to tell this man all that his writings had done for me. Lewis, The Great Divorce pp. 65-69.

to reproduce his original question, making a very providential mistake:

> *"So which of those is true:*
> *He's all-powerful and He cares, or...*
> *He cares and He's not all-powerful?"*

This was not the original question. Bashir's error came when he attempted to reproduce the first option, but this time he transposed it to "He's all-powerful and He cares..." A valid response to this would have been - "Yes...He's all-powerful *and* He cares." But such was not the case. Instead, Bell went on again with the same vacuous ramblings that are seen in his book, thereby revealing the utter bankruptcy of his theology. Bell has no real message of hope because he has abandoned the message of Christ's Gospel.

Clearly, Bell failed to present the message of Gospel-hope, but we ought to learn from such a moment. How should Christians respond to the crises and calamities of this world? One need not go very far on this matter by consulting Christ's response to two tragedies in His own day:

> Luke 13:1-5: 1. Now on the same occasion there were some present who reported to Him about the Galileans whose blood Pilate had mixed with their sacrifices. 2. And Jesus said to them, "Do you suppose that these Galileans were greater sinners than all other Galileans because they suffered this fate? 3. "I tell you, no, but unless you repent, you will all likewise perish. 4. "Or do you suppose that those eighteen on whom the tower in Siloam fell and killed them were worse culprits than all the men who live in Jerusalem? 5. "I tell you, no, but unless you repent, you will all likewise perish."

The message that Christ shares is very simple: *1. All have sinned and fall short of God's glory;*[194] *2. God graciously calls sinners to repent and live.*[195] None deserve such Gospel mercy, but all are called to it through the preaching of the Gospel.[196] Those who reject such a *caring* offer of grace and mercy are under the *all-powerful wrath and judgment* of God:

> John 3:36: "He who believes in the Son has eternal life; but he who does not obey the Son will not see life, but the wrath of God abides on him."

Despite the clear teachings of Scripture, Bell believes that *perishing* denotes a limited punishment that is designed to render a purgatorial restoration of the sinner - even in the afterlife. However, Christ clearly taught that the durative quality of Heaven and Hell are the same - *eternal, as seen in the parable of the sheep and the goats:*

> *Matthew 25:31-46: 31. "But when the Son of Man comes in His glory, and all the angels with Him, then He will sit on His glorious throne. 32. "All the nations will be gathered before Him; and He will separate*

---

[194] John 3:18: 18. "He who believes in Him is not judged; he who does not believe has been judged already, because he has not believed in the name of the only begotten Son of God, Romans 3:23: 23. for all have sinned and fall short of the glory of God.

[195] Ezekiel 18:32: 32. "For I have no pleasure in the death of anyone who dies," declares the Lord God. "Therefore, repent and live.", Luke 5:32: 32. "I have not come to call the righteous but sinners to repentance."

[196] Luke 24:46-47: 46. and He said to them, "Thus it is written, that the Christ would suffer and rise again from the dead the third day, 47. and that repentance for forgiveness of sins would be proclaimed in His name to all the nations, beginning from Jerusalem..

them from one another, as the shepherd separates the sheep from the goats; 33. and He will put the sheep on His right, and the goats on the left. 34. "Then the King will say to those on His right, 'Come, you who are blessed of My Father, inherit the kingdom prepared for you from the foundation of the world. 35. 'For I was hungry, and you gave Me something to eat; I was thirsty, and you gave Me something to drink; I was a stranger, and you invited Me in; 36. naked, and you clothed Me; I was sick, and you visited Me; I was in prison, and you came to Me.' 37. "Then the righteous will answer Him, 'Lord, when did we see You hungry, and feed You, or thirsty, and give You something to drink? 38. 'And when did we see You a stranger, and invite You in, or naked, and clothe You? 39. 'When did we see You sick, or in prison, and come to You?' 40. "The King will answer and say to them, 'Truly I say to you, to the extent that you did it to one of these brothers of Mine, even the least of them, you did it to Me.' 41. "Then He will also say to those on His left, 'Depart from Me, accursed ones, into the eternal fire which has been prepared for the devil and his angels; 42. for I was hungry, and you gave Me nothing to eat; I was thirsty, and you gave Me nothing to drink; 43. I was a stranger, and you did not invite Me in; naked, and you did not clothe Me; sick, and in prison, and you did not visit Me.' 44. "Then they themselves also will answer, 'Lord, when did we see You hungry, or thirsty, or a stranger, or naked, or sick, or in prison, and did not take care of You?' 45. "Then He will answer them, 'Truly I say to you, to the extent that you did not do it to one of the least of these, you did not do it to Me.' 46. "These will go away into eternal punishment, but the righteous into eternal life."

The conclusion of this parable is crucial, for it gives us a symmetry of thought concerning Heaven and Hell. The accusative/adjectival modifier is identical for *life* and *punishment* (Heaven and Hell): *they are eternal, indicative, realities:*

Matthew 25:46. "These will go away into eternal punishment, but the righteous into eternal life."

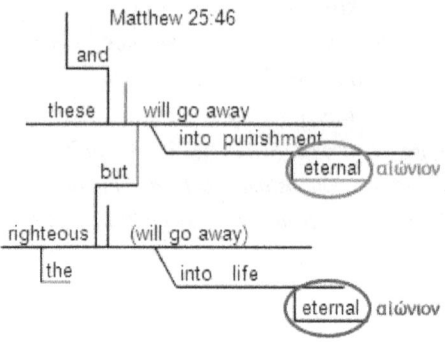

In all of this, we must behold the kindness *and* severity of God:[197] *"...unless you repent, you will all likewise perish."* Ultimately, the Good News is a message that is founded on some very bad news. The bad news is that *unless a sinner repents, he will likewise perish in his sin.* The good news is that *God is graciously calling men to turn to Him in faith.* The precious harmony of these messages, within the Gospel, reflects the same harmony of the Scriptural teaching on Heaven and Hell. To obfuscate the latter is to corrupt the former.

Bell may have capitalized on the opportunity to sell more books through his public interviews, but in the matter of sharing real Gospel hope to a watching world - he squandered such opportunities, and revealed nothing but the utter shame and bankruptcy of modern liberalism.

---

[197] Romans 11:22: Behold then the kindness and severity of God; to those who fell, severity, but to you, God's kindness, if you continue in His kindness; otherwise you also will be cut off.

APPENDIX

C.S. LEWIS AND THE USE OF LANGUAGE

"The Imaginative man in me...is more basic than either the religious writer or the critic."
- *C. S. Lewis, 1954*[198]

The language *and reasoning* of Scripture serves as an anchor for the Christian. Without such an anchor, we drift into the dangerous waters of our vain and perverse imaginations. In view of our examination of Lewis' treatment of scriptural language, I would submit to the reader that his example is one that should be avoided. His casual and *extrabiblical* treatment of the Greek words for love, in *The Four Loves,* provides a small example of this. The Christian needs the examples of better men for the present day; men like *John Bunyan*, whose writings are rich and profitable because, as Spurgeon said of him:

> "...this man is a living Bible! Prick him anywhere; his blood is Bibline, the very essence of the Bible flows from him. He cannot speak without quoting a text, for his very soul is full of the Word of God. I commend his example to you, beloved, and, still more, the example of our Lord Jesus. If the Spirit of God be in you, he will make you love the Word of God; and, if any of you imagine that the Spirit of God will lead you to dispense with the Bible, you are under the influence of another spirit which is not the Spirit of God at all. I trust that the Holy Spirit will endear to you every page of this Divine Record, so that you will feed upon it yourselves, and afterwards speak it out to others."[199]

---

[198] Packer, Surprised by Lewis, 1998.
[199] Charles Spurgeon, "The Last Words of Christ on the Cross," #2644, on Luke 23:46. *Metropolitan Tabernacle Pulpit* Volume 45.

Yet, the modern culture seems to be enamored with a different class of men. Those whose habit it is to venture away from the words and reasoning of Scripture are now in vogue, and even the use of disturbing, jolting, and profane speech has become the latest trend. Recently, I was reminded of this when speaking with a pastor friend of mine who was given the opportunity to teach the Scriptures at a local university. He called to ask for my thoughts about his discussion with various students over the use and meaning of various words. One of the students kept insisting that he had the freedom, in Christ, to use profane words – and he had no hesitation to identify those words in the hearing of the other students. His justification for his actions was not impressive, but he remained convinced of his "position."

Such is the progressive nature of modern Christendom.

I doubt that the Puritans of yesteryear would ever imagine the thought of "cursing pastors" and "cursing Christians" – but such is the brave new world of the religious culture today. I believe that the seeds of confusion in all of this go back even further to what has been a longstanding development of subjective religion here in America: a kind of modernized emotion-based-existentialism which subjugates everything beneath the thoughts, feelings, intentions, *and imaginations* of the worshipper: *the art and thought of man.* We have already addressed the problems with such subjectivism and must remember that everything in life is to be subject to God as that which is from Him, and through Him, and to Him – to Him be the glory forever, amen (Romans 11:36).

APPENDIX

This truth also applies to the very words that we use.

All the words we use, whether biblical or otherwise, should be offered as seasoned speech made useful for the edification or admonishment of others, for God's ultimate glory. But what we must understand is this: words have actual meaning, and are therefore not innately modified by our own subjective thoughts, feelings, or affections - even words like *erōs*. Now I should qualify this point as follows: a person's thoughts, feelings, and affections (or lack thereof) can influence the *impact* a word might have on the hearer. A man can say to his wife: "I love you," but with a drab spirit of indifference such a regurgitation will have no appeal. However, we must affirm, once again, that the innate meaning of his words are not at all changed by the reality of his indifference. In fact, the conflict between the word *love* and the man's shallow affections should remind us that words have concrete meanings. The good news within this illustration is that God's meaning and definition of love (H. *'āhāḇ*; G. *agapē*) stands as an objective reality despite the subjective corruption of men: the anchor of Scripture is never dragged away by the current of human thought. This understanding is crucial, but it is often lost within the world of subjective religion. With little or no objective anchor in God, the soul of man is lost within the morass of his own, ever-changing subjectivism, feelings, and thoughts. Paul addresses some of these issues when speaking of our use of words when he says:

> "Let no unwholesome word proceed from your mouth, but only such a word as is good for edification according to the need of the moment, so that it will give grace to those who hear." (Ephesians 4:29).

We should note that Paul does not say "Let no word be spoken unwholesomely" as if to place the emphasis on the way in which we speak. This would be a mere repetition of his earlier instructions in Ephesians 4:15 and 25 where Paul addresses the importance of the manner, intent, and affections of our communication. Verse 29, however, presses a distinct focus on the very words that we use. In fact, the nominative/adjectival construct is unmistakable: *logos sapros* (unwholesome words – or words that are rotten) vs. those "words that are good for edification." Paul's instruction is quite clear – it is not just *how we say things* that is important, but it is also *what we say* that is key, knowing that there are some things of which we should never speak:

> Ephesians 5:11-12: 11. Do not participate in the unfruitful deeds of darkness, but instead even expose them; 12. for it is disgraceful [*aischros*] even to speak of the things which are done by them in secret.

Some words and concepts are simply known to be *aischros* – utterly dark and disgraceful. Now imagine a member of the modern culture entering Paul's world for a minute. He might insist that Paul stand up, be a man, and talk about these dark and dirty things as a display of Christian maturity and stability – insisting that he is free and clear to do so on the grounds of a subjective innocence, replete with good intentions and affections. Paul's response would not change for a minute. He would simply respond by indicating that there are some things which are rotten (*sapros*) belonging in the waste-bin of language, and that it is disgraceful (*aischros*) – even ungracious (Ephesians 4:29) to allow such filth to pass the lips, no matter *how* we say it. To deny this is to play a rather dangerous word-game. Now, is there a subjective realm to this discussion? Are there not words that are somewhat "borderline" on the issue of unwholesome speech? Certainly, but remember, even the world knows (for the most part) what profanity is. If you are in doubt of this, try reading a movie review sometime and you will find that even the inhabitants of Hollywood understand the theology of unwholesome speech well enough. Clearly, Paul didn't give his audience a list of things that are "disgraceful even to speak of" – such an act would be a self-contradiction within his own letter. Nor did he give us a Mishnaic listing of unwholesome words – he clearly understood that this is not a matter that can be reduced to superficial legalism.

As the children of God we must be so invested in learning the things that are pleasing to God (objectively)[200] that our walk will take us away from the unwholesomeness of this world. Therefore, we do not walk about with lengthy lists of prohibited words, instead, we are called to exercise sound judgment, self-control, and discernment in this matter of the use of our tongues, knowing that we will at times stumble and err as mere men (James 3:2). However, if we are invested in this matter of speaking the truth in love (Ephesians 4:15), then all of these other conflicts will diminish beneath the weightiness of God's immeasurable grace (Ephesians 4:29).

It is crucial that we consider our own subjective affections and attitudes when speaking, for "the mouth speaks out of that which fills the heart" (Matthew 12:34). Yet, our subjective

---

[200] Ephesians 5:7-10

thoughts and feelings cannot be our chief end. Instead, we must look objectively outside of ourselves, and remember that the very words that we use have meaning – some good; some bad – and that our intentions do not transform the innate reality of such meaning. Overall, our heart matters; our words matter; and everything ought to be laid before the Lord for His ultimate glory. Particularly in the matter of our speech, such subjectivism has the tendency to exalt one's own intentions, thoughts, and feelings over the objective realities of language and communication. Therefore, my own thoughts and feelings do not modify the *innate* meaning of words; even though they might affect the *impact* that such words have on others (as in the illustration of a heartless husband who professes to love his wife). As previously noted, Paul was not only concerned about our subjective motives when speaking,[201] but he was also concerned about the very words that we use;[202] understanding that some things should never pass the lips of God's children.[203] In these examples it is evident that Paul is speaking of language that is expressly *secular*, rather than *biblical*, otherwise we would have to conclude that there are some aspects of Scripture that should never be repeated - *may it never be (2 Timothy 3:16)!* This distinction is, I believe, important, especially if we are to learn about how we can properly season our speech with the salt of genuine wisdom.[204] The Scriptures themselves offer the Christian a very real anchor to all reality and meaning in life; without which, we have no real "salt" to season our speech.

---

[201] Eph. 4:15, 25.

[202] Eph. 4:29.

[203] Eph. 5:12

[204] Colossians 4:6: Let your speech always be with grace, as though seasoned with salt, so that you will know how you should respond to each person.

We as Christians, of all people, should be the most cautious about such matters, knowing that the weapons of our warfare are powerful for the tearing down of the false fortresses of this world's thoughts, words, and ideas. As previously cited:

> *2 Corinthians 10:3-5: 3. For though we walk in the flesh, we do not war according to the flesh, 4. for the weapons of our warfare are not of the flesh, but divinely powerful for the destruction of fortresses. 5. We are destroying speculations and every lofty thing raised up against the knowledge of God, and we are taking every thought captive to the obedience of Christ*

Remember that the building materials employed by the world against the knowledge of God are *logismous - faulty reasoning/speculations* and *hupsoma epairōmenon - lofty expressions of arrogance;* and the divinely powerful weaponry that has been given to us to tear down such fortresses is *the knowledge of God as supplied in God's Word - the sword of the Spirit.*[205] The Christian must never underestimate the importance of Scripture and *scriptural language* - even down to the last *jot and tittle*. Without the *sword of the Spirit* (in all of its precious detail) our words are reduced to dull and useless instruments; but with the whole counsel of God's Word (in all of its precious detail) we have a substantial means of engaging this world.

This principle sounds easy enough, but the application can be rather challenging.

---

[205] Eph. 6:17

Having been raised in southern California, I am reminded of the frequent habit of young people who use the word *righteous* as a synonym for the word *cool*. Even the word *awesome* is also used in this vein. Such a casual and trite usage of these words is degrading to their root meanings and identities. A Toyota vehicle may be an impressive piece of machinery, but it is not *awesome* (awe/fear inspiring) *per se*.[206] Obviously, the world uses language in often base and useless ways, and it frequently invokes the Lord's name in vain as further proof of its disregard for God-centered discourse. However, as the children of God, we must not follow the world's lead - even if it *feels* "cool" and "hip." The theological shock-jocks of the modern day are not helping the church in this matter, especially when they venture outside the beauty and purity of Scripture. Neither profanity, ambiguous/shocking statements, or poetic pithiness should ever serve to supplant the clear and perspicuous message of Scripture.

Let me illustrate this matter as follows: I often use the expression - "godly jealousy" in order to describe my zeal for the priority of the Gospel. Now I ask the reader: Is this a meaningful expression? Am I being a theological shock-jock by using such language, and should a Christian ever be "jealous" since James says "...you are envious [*zēloutē - jealous*] and cannot obtain; so you fight and quarrel" - which is exactly what we see when the Jews of Thessalonica became jealous [*zēlosantēs*] and formed an angry mob against the Christians?[207] As well, since God

---

[206] In Scripture God's name, deeds, and judgment are called, appropriately, *awesome*.

[207] 1 Corinthians 13:4: 4. Love is patient, love is kind and is not jealous; love does not brag and is not arrogant,

declares Himself to be a jealous God who shares His glory with no one,[208] am I at liberty to use such a word for myself as an expression of *godly* affections? The only reason why my answer is *yes* is because the Apostle Paul himself used this expression in order to convey his godly zeal for those within the Corinthian church who were being led astray by false teachers.[209] In fact, the use of such a biblical expression affords me the opportunity to explain myself *from the text of Scripture* such that the hearer is led away from what could become *my theology* to that of *God and His truth*.

Now, how about the word lust? Would it be scripturally meaningful to employ the word lust - maybe *godly lust* - in order to describe an earnest desire for something good?

Answer: *no.*

While I have never heard a theologian try to foist the exact expression, *godly lust,* into the shock-jock lexicon, I offer it here as a generic illustration for your consideration (and perhaps to preempt any future attempts for someone to do so). In the English, the word *lust* converges to this idea of sinful affections. As it is used in English translations of the Bible, there is no use of the word *lust* in connection with godly desire. For someone to try to use such a term for its shock value, as in the case of *godly lust*, I would suggest that they are pointedly disparaging *scripturally grounded word meanings* in order to draw some form of attention to their teaching. But James reminds his

---

[208] Exodus 20:3-5
[209] 2 Corinthians 11:1-4.

audience: "...you *lust*[210] and do not have; so you commit murder..." (James 4:2). And why is this so? James queries further: "What is the source of quarrels and conflicts among you? Is not the source your pleasures[211] that wage war in your members?" (James 4:1). When people hear the English word *lust*, there should be no ambiguity in their understanding of the term. Should we misuse the term at all, we produce a form of confusion that should not at all exist. When Scriptural language converges to a fairly monolithic meaning, we dull the blade of Holy Writ through a misuse of such important terms. And while such tactics may garner the attention of others, we must ask the question: *who is ultimately getting that attention?* In the introduction of this book, we consulted J.C. Ryle for his wisdom on the dangers of seeking theological novelty. Here, we should look at what he says about the dangers of using *novel words and expressions*:

> "Finally, I must deprecate, and I do it in love, the use of uncouth and new-fangled terms and phrases in teaching sanctification. I plead that a movement in favor of holiness cannot be advanced by new-coined phraseology, or by disproportioned and one-sided statements--or by overstraining and isolating particular texts--or by exalting one truth at the expense of another--or by allegorizing and accommodating texts, and squeezing out of them meanings which the Holy Spirit never put in them--or by speaking contemptuously and bitterly of those who do not entirely see things with our eyes, and do not work exactly in our ways. These things do not make for peace: they rather repel many and keep them at a distance. The cause of true sanctification is not helped, but hindered, by such

---

[210] G. *epithumea:* This word can be used for either *godly desire* or *lust*, depending on the context.
[211] G. *hēdonēn*.

APPENDIX

weapons as these. A movement in aid of holiness which produces strife and dispute among God's children is somewhat suspicious. For Christ's sake, and in the name of truth and charity, let us endeavor to follow after peace as well as holiness. 'What God has joined together let not man put asunder.' It is my heart's desire, and prayer to God daily, that personal holiness may increase greatly among professing Christians in England. But I trust that all who endeavor to promote it will adhere closely to the proportion of Scripture, will carefully distinguish things that differ, and will separate 'the precious from the vile.' (Jeremiah 15:19.)"[212]

Ryle's wisdom is timeless, helpful, and should not be easily dismissed in the present day - *because it is biblical.* Clearly, Ryle's battle of yesteryear is the battle of the modern day, because *nothing is new under the sun.* His warning for his generation is for us as well. We all misspeak at times,[213] and our vocabulary will continue to be refined and transformed[214] as the Lord sanctifies us; but the direction that we must seek is one which *presses back* to the ancient anchor of Holy Writ, rather than forward to this ever-changing and dying world. May the Lord season our speech for our good and His ultimate glory.

---

[212] Ryle, Holiness, p. XXIX.
[213] James 3:2-3.
[214] Romans 12:1-2.

INDEX

'āhāḇ, 54
Abraham, 45, 90, 105
Affections

   Godly, 78, 80, 135
Afterlife, 91, 115, 118-119, 124
agapē, 39, 40, 57, 62, 64, 67, 68, 72, 76, 81
Alexander, 114
Allegory, 32
anothen, 55
Areopagus, 27
Athena, 28
Athens,, 27, 66
Bashir, Martin, 122, 123
Bell, Rob

   Love Wins, 10, 18, 27, 83, 86, 87, 92, 95, 96, 98, 100, 112, 113, 114, 115, 116, 117, 118, 119, 120, 121

   Video, 10
Buddhism, 46, 116
Bunyan, John, 127
Campolo, Tony, 105
Christ

   Atonement, 17, 116, 118

   Bride of, 20

   Penal Substitution, 17, 121

   Union with, 72, 78, 84

Christendom, Contemporary, 22
Christian

   Affections, 23
Dante, 14
Darth Vader, 114
Decalogue, 30
Demons, 61
Doctrine

   Uncertainty, 25-27, 35, 115
Double Standard, 11
eḥāḏ, 48
elōhiym, 45
Ecstasy, 39, 74, 78, 79
Emergent Church, 10, 26, 113
Eminem, 119
enthumeseōs, 31
erōs, 38, 39, 53, 60-70, 72-78, 81, 84

   Corinthian Church, 75

   Dionysus, 78

   Fertility Cults, 79

   Marriage, 75
Esau, 23, 24
Eternity, 26
Evangelicalism, 11
Exegesis, 30, 114, 118
exegēsato, 30
Extrabiblical Reasoning, 25-27, 35
Festivals, 71, 75, 78

INDEX

Foremost Commandment, 43-44, 49-50, 56, 62, 72, 80
Free Will, 20, 23, 61, 89, 100
Gandhi, 106, 108
genēthē, 55
George MacDonald, 11, 18, 22, 24, 43, 94, 106, 112, 122
Gerontius, Dream of, 14
God

  Creator, 29

  Deemed Untrustworthy, 93

  Despot, 29

  Divine Nature, 17-18, 28-30, 66, 87, 92, 95, 100, 115, 120

  Free-will, 17

  Grace of, 18, 83, 88, 120

  His Singularity, 48

  His Supremacy, 48

  Holy Spirit, The, 35, 54, 79, 102, 127

  Justice, 94

  Mercy of, 46, 94, 105, 116, 124

  Providence, 86

  Sovereign Freedom, 18, 45

  Sovereignty, 17, 87

  Triune Love, 81

  Unknown God, 60, 67, 84
Gospel, 29, 46, 65, 66, 84, 98, 101-106, 109, 116, 123, 124, 126, 134

  Solemnity, 101-106, 109
Graeco-Roman world, 29, 53, 65-66, 71, 80
Greek

  Art and Thought of, 28, 30, 31, 43, 58, 66, 95

  Artisans, 30

  Love of *par excellence*, 65

  Philosophers, 27

  Spirits, 30
Hades, 105
HarperOne, 10, 115
Heaven, 10, 17, 23, 86, 90, 91, 95, 98, 101, 113, 120-121, 124-126
Hell, 7, 10, 17, 18, 22-23, 86, 89, 90-92, 95, 97-98, 100, 101, 105-106, 113, 115, 117-119, 122, 124-126

  Chasm, 90, 105

  Torment, 91, 93-94, 105
Hermes, 66
Hitchens, Christopher, 95-97
ḥesed, 94
hēdonē, 69, 72, 79
Holy Spirit

  Fruit of, 56

Humanity
- Nonentity, 92
- Shrinking, 92

Humility, 27

Hymenaeus, 74, 114

Idolatry, 28, 66, 67

Japan, Crisis in, 122

Jealousy
- Godly, 134

Jesus Christ, 29, 30, 46, 97, 102

Judgment
- Sheep and the Goats, 124

Julian, Lady, 26

Kempis, Thomas, 41

Lazarus, 90, 105

Lewis, Clive Staples, 1, 3-4, 7, 10-11, 13, 16-18, 22-26, 38-40, 42-43, 46-47, 52-53, 55, 60-64, 75, 81, 86, 89, 91, 98, 105-106, 112, 116, 122, 127
- Chronicles of Narnia, the, 24
- Four Loves, The, 23, 38, 39, 40-43, 47, 52, 53, 55, 60, 62, 63, 127
- Imaginative Man, 26, 31
- On MacDonald's Teaching, 25
- The Great Divorce, 13, 22, 25-27, 86-87, 89, 91, 106, 112, 122

Lord's Table, The, 76

Love
- "Greatest Love of All", 38
- Alien Affection, 54
- Basis of Redemption, 56
- Centrality to Christian Life, 56
- Christian Fellowship, 56
- Christian Witness, 56
- Christ's Control, 77
- Demands Freedom, 17, 86
- Endures all Things, 78
- First-Fruit of the Spirit, 56
- Humility, 77, 134
- Kindness, 76
- Marriage, 56
- Patience, 76
- Rejoices in Truth, 77
- Self-Esteem, 38, 39, 72, 84
- Trinitarian, 79
- Worship, 56

Lust, 54, 69, 135-136

MacDonald, George, 16, 18, 20, 24-26, 43, 93-94, 106, 122

   Lewis' "Master", 24

   Unspoken Sermons, 25, 94

Mankind

   Children of Wrath, 35

   Depravity, 17, 68, 88

   Extrabiblical Reasoning, 57

   Freedom, 18, 87, 88, 89, 115

   Free-will, 17, 22

   Human Wisdom, 35

   Man-Centered, 58

   Works-Righteousness, 45, 49

Marriage, 56, 74

McLaren, Brian, 105, 106

Minucius Felis, 71

Mishnah, 131

Mythological Genealogy, 69

Mythology, 64-67

National TV, 122

Nero, 71

New Covenant, 47

Newman, Cardinal John Henry, 14

Olympus, 28

Origen, 68, 118, 119

Orthodox Christianity, 115, 120

Paganism, 53, 65

Papal Encyclical, 60, 64

Paul, Apostle, 20, 27, 33, 96, 135

Pederasty, 62

Personal Ecstasy, 71

philos, 39, 40, 69

philostorgē, 39

Pithiness, *134*

Pope Benedict XVI, 60, 64

Preacher

   as a Foolish Jokester, 103

   as a Grave Person, 104

Presumption, 10, 64

Pride, 31, 34, 60

Prodigal Son, *91*

Profanity, 134

Purgatory, 12, 14

Puritans, 128

Reconciliation

   Postmortem, 17, 22

   Potential, 17

   Purgatorial, 17, 22, 91-92, 115, 118-120, 124

Relational Indifference, 60

Resurrection, 97

Rich Man, the, 90-91, 105

Roman Catholic, 12, 60

Satan, 61, 114, 119

Scripture, 4, 17, 20, 29, 31, 40, 46, 57, 60, 66, 95, 100-101, 113, 124, 132-134

Divine Revelation, 27, 43, 46

   Inerrancy, 17

   Reasoning from, 18

   Sola Scriptura, 29

   White Spaces, 100

Self-Gratification, 69
Selfishness, 60, 67, 78, 84
Senecca, 75
Septuagint, 68
Shock-Jock, 134-135
Subjectivism, 132
tabula rasa, 28, 67
technēs, 31
Theology

Open Theism, 87, 121
Ungodliness, 29
Universalism, 10, 11, 25, 26, 115, 116, 120, 121

   Inclusivism, 116

   Universal Opportunity, 46, 116

Unwholesome Words, 130
Varro, 70
Worship, 28, 29, 30, 31, 47, 48, 54, 55, 72, 74, 75, 76, 78, 84
Zeal

   Religious, 28

Zeus, 28, 66

Proverbs 3:5-18:

5 Trust in Jehovah with all thy heart,
And lean not upon thine own understanding:
6 In all thy ways acknowledge him, And he will direct thy paths.
7 Be not wise in thine own eyes; Fear Jehovah, and depart from
evil: 8 It will be health to thy navel, And marrow to thy bones. 9
Honor Jehovah with thy substance, And with the first-fruits of
all thine increase: 10 So shall thy barns be filled with plenty, And
thy vats shall overflow with new wine. 11 My son, despise not
the chastening of Jehovah; Neither be weary of his reproof: 12
For whom Jehovah loveth he reproveth; Even as a father the son
in whom he delighteth. 13 Happy is the man that findeth
wisdom, And the man that getteth understanding. 14 For the
gaining of it is better than the gaining of silver, And the profit
thereof than fine gold. 15 She is more precious than rubies: And
none of the things thou canst desire are to be compared unto
her. 16 Length of days is in her right hand; In her left hand are
riches and honor. 17 Her ways are ways
of pleasantness, And all her
paths are peace.
18 She is a
tree of life
to them that
lay hold
upon her:
And happy
is every
one that
retaineth
her.

www.ingramcontent.com/pod-product-compliance
Lightning Source LLC
Chambersburg PA
CBHW020005050426
42450CB00005B/326